Project Planning and Management

Project Planning and Management

Ad van der Weide
Adrie Beulens
Stephan van Dijk

Lemma Publishers – Utrecht – 2003

ISBN 90 5931 152 3
NUR 801

http://www.lemma.nl
infodesk@lemma.nl

© 2003 LEMMA Publishers, P.O. Box 3320, 3502 GH UTRECHT, the Netherlands

Cover design and typography: Twin Design BV, Culemborg, the Netherlands

Preface

Before you is a book on the subject of project planning and management with an unorthodox and refreshing approach in which innovative ideas are combined with a high degree of practicality. Experienced managers will recognise that decades of practical experience have gone into the writing of the book. Students will appreciate the clearness of the approach and ease of use of the methods and tools. Hopefully, the authors have succeeded in their mission to integrate practical and theoretical insights and diverse project management tools into a comprehensive, effective, and efficient approach for the management and planning of projects, applicable for a large range of projects, from small one-off research projects to very large multi-staged ICT projects.

A unique aspect of the approach is the firm embedding of projects within the context of the companies in which they reside and in their objectives to generate business value. Unlike many books and readings on project planning and management, projects are not seen in this book as being detached from their company. In the first chapter, the authors extensively explore the values that a project must deliver to a company and all its stakeholders. Without a clear understanding of the business values, the project's successful completion is jeopardised. Here the authors incorporate common business sense and wider notions on strategic management and business values as developed by Porter (1985), Kaplan (1990) and Hammer and Champy (1993).

Another unique aspect of the approach is the focus on effective people management and intra-project communication. Many books on project management concentrate on the tools for project planning and monitoring and underestimate the importance of people and people management. The authors take the view that people are a main source of innovation and a main foundation of an organisation's competitive advantage. Careful development of the organisation's 'social capital' (people, knowledge, and capabilities) is therefore of crucial importance. As projects are excellent opportunities for learning, specific attention is paid to the integration of in-team doing, coaching, and learning and into the promotion of self-regulating teams to increase the rate of learning and the pleasure of working in projects.

Still another main subject is the planning, monitoring, and control of projects. The authors have enhanced the common approach to project planning by applying the concept of realising business values into project planning. Project break-down approaches are introduced that facilitate the reduction of project complexity, hence providing the flexibility to maximise the chances to produce project outputs, and therefore business values, to specifications, and on time. The reader will become aware of several approaches to the design of activities and interfaces and of their specific consequences. Planning focuses upon the clever design of 'interfaces' between activities rather than upon the design of the activities themselves. Well-designed interfaces are valuable intermediate products that not only represent business values but also reduce project coordination efforts.

In short: The book's aim is to give the reader a concise account of the many aspects of project management and planning. It makes him aware of the fact that projects cannot be managed properly without a clear understanding of the company and of the business values of the project outputs and of the stakeholders/receivers of these. Further, it emphasises the necessity of complexity management, careful planning, and effective people management.

The approach adopted here, will help the reader to survive in the complicated world of the project management.

The book will be of use to students, consultants, managers, scientists, and all other people who are involved in projects or project management, in business, research corporations, or governmental institutions.

Contents

Introduction

This book was originally written for **Wageningen** University's Project Planning and Management (PPM) course and workshops used in preparing students for careers in commerce and industry. Since 2003, the course is included in the Master-degree programme of the university.

The human aspects of projects such as conflict handling, chairing meetings, manager-associate communication, and team building are not specifically addressed, although they unavoidably appear throughout the book. The book contains appendices for presentations and communication, all focussing on effectiveness.

The objective of this book is to prepare students for future job situations such that they can contribute confidently and effectively when working on projects or managing project teams.

A project is a one-off, independent process and has the objective of creating a predefined result.

Experienced scientific researchers observe that projects are a common part of their work and being a good project manager and a good team member helps them in their careers as well as in their scientific achievements. The probability that students in their Masters degree will be required to manage projects is quite high.

Observations and comments from students of Wageningen University who have used syllabus versions considerably helped to improve the practicality of this book.

Chapters 1-6 relate to items concerning project planning and management while Chapter 7 is devoted to handling the process of a project.

The best way to read this book is:
1   Section 1.1-1.4;
2   Glance through Chapter 7; the process of a project;
3   Read the remainder of Chapter 1;
4   Read Chapters 2-6;
5   Read Chapter 7 again.

In Chapter 1 (Definition), we define a project and its objectives within the context of a company or other type of large entity that the project is part of. Large entities are structured predominantly to facilitate repetitive processes. A project is an incidental process that must find a route through that same structure. Like any change in an organisation, a project is likely to encounter resistance.

In Chapter 2 (Project management), we define project management and its responsibilities and tasks. The liaison that must take place between a project and a company (or other large entity) is explained and management roles towards people, performance, quality, and costs (consumption of resources) are worked out.

In Chapter 3 (Planning), we propose methods and techniques for effective project planning. We explain how a project can be decomposed into executable parts and how to design efficient interfaces between them that reduce complexity without creating extra work. We go into work breakdown structures, consecutive and parallel running, critical paths, milestones, and liaison with outside parties. Further, we discuss project-planning software.

In chapter 4 (Monitoring and Control), we propose methods for effectively monitoring and controlling the use of resources. This entails planned and actual associate-time usage, budgeted and actual costs, and planned and actual usage of other resources. There are also sections on cash and quality management.

In Chapter 5 (Progress Reporting and Communication), we discuss line-communication and reporting. The main elements are planned and actual output deliveries, budgets, actual costs and revised estimates at completion, planned and required cash, and quality reporting.

In Chapter 6 (Success and Failure), we present some practical project management experiences such as what works well and what does not, reasons for failure and reasons for success. We go, in more detail, into reasons why there is resistance to change and ways to cope with it.

In Chapter 7 (Project Sequence Model) all the elements from the previous chapters are brought together into a model that enables the project manager and his team to structure and sequence the main steps of a project. We start with project orientation and assignment because that is the first step towards ensuring a proper mandate and achievable objectives. The steps to follow are proposal, preparation, execution, implementation, and termination, follow-up and evaluation.

The correct reference to the project manager or to a project team member is 'he or she' and 'his or her'. In this book, they are often referred to in the male forms of 'he' and 'his' only. In no way should this be interpreted as a lack of respect or appreciation for females in these roles. It just made a couple of hundred sentences a little shorter and a bit more readable.

1 Definition

Learning objectives

The purpose of this chapter is to clarify the role and the positioning of a project within the context of a company (or other type of larger entity) and its stakeholders.

After reading this chapter, the reader should have improved his general understanding of projects, their roles, and their impacts on organisations. He or she will be in a better position to recognise the company requirements for a project.

The chapter contains the authors' objectives for Project Planning and Management (PPM) followed throughout the book. The importance of project management in future job situations of students is emphasised. Projects are placed within the context of the company, the institute, or some other type of entity that they form part of and for which they must generate value. The purpose of a project is stated in its mission. A vision translates that mission into clear points and helps in creating a strategy for the project. The organisation structures of large entities are, in general, rather fixed, although focussing predominantly on facilitating repetitive processes. A project is an incidental process that must force a route through that same structure. Projects have impact on people and can trigger resistance.

1.1 The objectives

The main objective is to prepare students for future job situations so that they can contribute confidently and effectively when working on projects or managing project teams.

Note: The probability that a Master degree student will encounter projects in his future job is high. Given his relatively high education level, it is also likely that in future jobs he will be asked to plan and manage projects.

In past courses, some students have argued that, because they are educated to become scientific researchers, they do not expect to be involved in projects. That is a serious misjudgement. Experienced scientific researchers observe, time and time again, that projects are a common part of their work and being a good project manager and a good project team member helps them in their careers as well as in their scientific achievements.

1.2 Definitions and the context of a project

A project is a one-off process and has the objective of creating a predefined result.

Kramers Dutch translation dictionary defines a *company* as an independent economic entity with the objective of making profit. Within the context of this book, we define a company as a network of interacting processes with the objective to satisfy the needs of its stakeholders. This redefinition serves to put emphasis on two important principles:

1 To make profit is not only the objective of the shareholders but also that of all the other stakeholders (*stakeholder principle*).

2 Profit is expressed not only in financial terms but also in many other types of value (*value principle*).

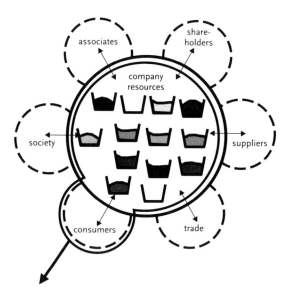

Figure 1.1 Buckets model
Stakeholders, see, e.g. Kaplan, 1990; Mitroff, 1983; Freeman 1984.

Stakeholders are all the partners of a company 'who have a stake in the company'. In terms of this book, stakeholders are grouped into six headings (Figure 1.1).

Consumer (A person who buys and 'consumes' products in the meaning as being the end station, not forwarding products to a next value-adding partner. Consumer includes also the gatekeeper and the individual who buys for another consumer.) In the example of a dog food company, the consumer includes the dog, the child who is the dog's boss and the mother who buys the dog food.

The *consumer chain* is the (network of) series of consecutive processes in cooperating companies that produce a consumer product (inversed direction demand chain). A simple representation of the dog food chain encompasses the producers of raw materials (farmers), slaughterhouses, food producers, canners and packagers, marketers, wholesalers, and retailers. The reality will be much more complicated and encompass a network of supply chains that provision the animal food chain, such as a breeder chain, a fodder chain, an energy chain and a packaging materials chain.

Customer. The retailer or trade partner whose position in the consumer chain sits between the company and the consumer. In the example of a company that manufactures dog food, the wholesalers and retailers are customers.

17

Supplier. The partner that precedes the company in the consumer chain. In the example of a company that manufactures dog food, suppliers include a large range of partners such as raw material suppliers, suppliers of cans, jars, and printed labels, but also the suppliers of energy, engineering firms, office stationary and outsourcing or contracting agencies.

Associate. The company staff, including contracted, in-sourced people. Associate represents all persons providing labour or human capacity to the company. Associate means people of all ranks who perform work in the company. It also includes persons with limited duration contracts.

Shareholder. The supplier of risk-taking capital. The owner or co-owner of the company or the holder of shares.

Society. Authorities, environment, social and business organisations. Examples encompass a large range of partners who often interact with a company on behalf of, and representing, groups of people. Think of the city office, institutes for common services, trades unions, sports clubs and national, regional, and local governmental bodies. Also fauna and flora can be seen as belonging to society.

Note that company partners can belong to more than one stakeholder group. For instance, an associate who owns shares in a company is also a shareholder and if he also buys the company's products, he is also a consumer. Similarly, a supplier can also be a customer or a society partner. An in-sourced contractor fits into the meaning of associate as well as supplier.

Products represent all the exchanges that take place between stakeholders and the company. Products are carriers of value and can be concrete or abstract. They are the goods, raw materials, and services, as well as the information, knowledge, expertise, capabilities, options and ideas. Products are produced in processes.

A *process* is the function of turning an agreement with a stakeholder into a delivered product and a received reward. In each process, one can distinguish the following four main sub-processes or steps:

1   negotiate   (= sell);
2   design   (= develop);
3   produce   (= make);
4   distribute and receive payment   (= deliver and collect).

A *procedure* describes a process in terms of tasks and their (precedence) relationships. It is the way in which a process runs through the organisation. The process is broken down in order to facilitate assigning tasks to persons in the company. In function-oriented organisations, the process is broken down into functional tasks that can be allocated to function specialists or function departments. A procedure is a choice 'to run the process through the organisation at a certain point in time'. The procedure can change, while the process remains the same.

In terms of the principles of this book, a procedure should not just define tasks but first of all, also the outputs (products) from the tasks. They are intermediate products or components of the eventual process output.

Value is the appreciation of a product or resource. It is the perception of the owner of a resource or the receiver of a product. The provider of a product defines the costs but cannot define the value for the receiver. The costs are the provider's perception of the value of the resources he used in order to produce the product.

Profit is the value surplus between products received from and products delivered to the stakeholders.

Resources are the materials, machines, people, money, information, knowledge, skills, and all the other deployable elements in a company. Resources are the carriers of value.

Interfacing is the execution of the coordination between parts of a process, e.g. between the sub processes and tasks in a process. *Interfaces* are intermediate products that are forwarded between the parts. They are the connectors as well as the components of the final product from the process.

Effectiveness is value generated over investments from all resources.

Production is products produced per time.

Productivity is products produced per person (sometimes per machine) per time.

Efficiency is efforts per product.

> **Example**
> Production, productivity, efficiency, value and effectiveness
> A process in which 10 persons produce 10 items per day.
> If two persons are added and then produce 12 items per day, production is deemed to have improved.
> If the 10 items per day are being produced with eight persons, then productivity has improved because products per person per day have increased from 10/10 to 10/8.
> If the total usage of resources per product has reduced, then efficiency has improved. That can be achieved by reducing person time, material usage, machine time, or the use of facilities.
> If the customer is willing to pay more (return more value) per product, then value has improved. That is also the case when the product is not for a customer but for another stakeholder, e.g. a supplier 'pays' more with cheaper supplies but also in other ways such as loyalty, speed of response, and added information.
> If the value returned for a product increases and/or resource usage by product reduces, then effectiveness has increased.

Alternative and/or enhancing definitions:
- Efficiency means performing a given task as well as possible in relation to some predefined performance criteria.
- Effectiveness involves identifying what should be done and ensuring that the chosen criterion is the relevant one.
- Effectiveness: better fulfilment of the needs of the recipient of the product.
- Effectiveness requires adaptation and learning, at the risk of redundancy and false starts.
- Efficiency involves a narrowing of focus and minimisation of the time, cost, and/or effort required to carry out a given activity (Keen and Scott Morton, 1978).

1.3 Example projects, example companies and other entities

Projects:
- re-open the IJsselmeer to the open sea;
- write a manuscript;
- design a production process for solar-driven lawn mowers;
- do a survey of citizens' satisfactions of municipal services;
- do a benchmark of financial services;
- develop a new drug;
- develop a new brake for a caterpillar vehicle;
- research methods for measuring radioactive contamination in the Barents Sea;
- research literature for brake systems;
- build a house;
- make a business plan;
- execute a business plan;
- redecorate an office;
- make a trip around the world in a 12-meter yacht;
- find a solution to purify and recycle wastewater at carwash sites;
- develop a solution to reduce algae in the inner waters;
- do the weather forecasts for the sailing race around the world;
- design and develop a course for project planning and management;
- re-organise a department;
- make a human resources development plan;
- design a quality certification process for the pig-meat chain;
- research the effectiveness of pig pedigrees for mass meat production;
- make an inventory of harvesting robots.

Companies:
- a one-man business
  The simplest form of a company. The associate is also the shareholder. Take the example of a self-employed programmer. He sells his time to companies needing programming capacity for a fee and makes a financial profit if his income is higher than his costs. But he may decide to offer his time for a far lower fee if he feels that he can learn something of great value. He still makes a profit although not in monetary terms.
- an independent advisor
- the United Nations
  The United Nations also has the objective of making a profit. This profit is expressed predominantly in terms such as conflict prevention, global regulations and agreements, and the organisation of economic aid. In terms of money, the UN has the objective of not spending more than it receives. It has a money profit target of zero.
- Royal Dutch Airlines (KLM)
- The co-operation agreement of KLM, Northwest Airlines and their partners
- A university
- A big international company
- An initiative of financiers to build the tunnel between Dover and Calais
- Netherlands Management Co-operation Program (NMCP)
  This institute sends out experts to developing countries to help with projects and with the added assignment of building up valuable knowledge and skills in that country. The experts give their time and efforts for free. Also they make a profit, but it is not in monetary terms. They may perceive a value because they gain new friendships, learn about foreign countries, of the pleasure simply in doing good work, are honoured that they were asked or genuinely believe in a life hereafter where they will be rewarded.
- the Defence Department
  The defence department is part of the government and has been assigned defence tasks on behalf of the nation. Its profit target in money terms is zero because it cannot spend more than it receives. The defence department receive tax money and deploys that in order to generate resources such as well-equipped and well-trained troops. It provides the capability to defend against aggressors. Its stakeholders, e.g. the citizens, perceive a value: that of protection.
- Greenpeace
- a water purification plant
- city government
- a travel agency

1.4 Project impact on companies

The three most important ways of how projects have impact on a company:

1 Projects can make a part of a process that runs completely inside a company and consists of several projects. In order to understand the role of such a project, the project team must understand the whole process, which means tracing the process back to the originator, pursuing it to the final project, and identifying the stakeholders and the products exchange.

2 Projects can consist of a complete stakeholder process. Beginning with an agreement with the stakeholder and ending with delivering the agreed product and receiving the agreed rewards. Such a project is self-sufficient. The project contains all the essentials for understanding its role.

3 Projects can be part of a process spanning several companies. In this case, the project team must first understand the role of the total chain process, in terms of understanding the stakeholder and the product exchange with that stakeholder. Next, stakeholders must understand the role of their project and their company in that process.

Any activity must eventually deliver value to stakeholders. And at the very end there must be products for a consumer who is willing to buy them. The route

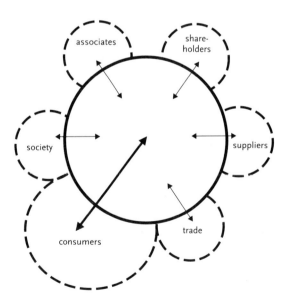

Figure 1.2 Products for the consumer

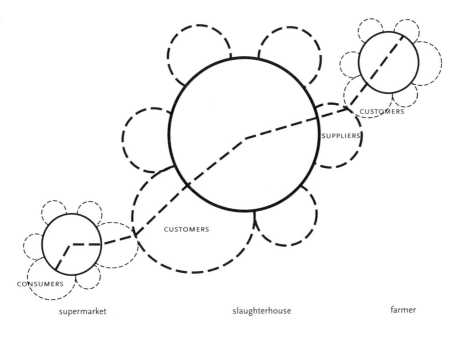

Figure 1.3 One project passing through several companies

to the stakeholder is sometimes not so obvious to a person working on a project that is only a small and remote element in a long chain.

Examples of a project that delivers a product directly to the consumer (Figure 1.2): to develop a new drug, create an information site on the Internet.

The example pictured in Figure 1.3 is a quality certification project in a meat chain. The entire chain is involved and it ends with the consumer.

Similar projects: to develop a registration system for horses, set up an integrated distribution system for transplant organs. Develop a planning model for land-usage in the Sahel. To build a house: a chain of projects that runs through architect, site-preparation, construction, electrical installation, plumbers and decorators.

Most common, however, is that a project is a part of a chain inside the company (Figure 1.4).

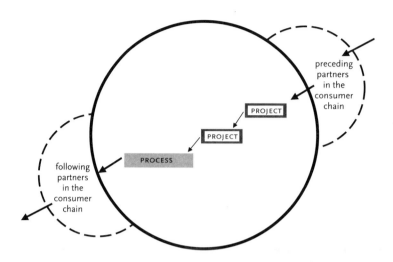

Figure 1.4   The project is part of a chain within the company

Examples

To investigate lung infections in pig stocks, to develop a salary system, to do a product survey, to organise an office move, to do a benchmark, to train a department, to install a new cabling network, to review the efficiency of a technique, to carry out a reorganisation.

Also, a project to make a proposal for another project, a feasibility study for a survey, and the implementation of a plan made in a previous project. The creation of a new production line delivers value to a shareholder. A follow-up process 'to produce products on that line' connects the project with the consumer.

1.5   A project, an incident in a fixed organisation

In contemporary society there are very few self-sufficient jobs. Most workers must operate within the context of a larger entity such as a company, an institute, a university, a co-operation agreement with a number of partners, or whatever other contexts are possible. Here we shall use company as the representative of any such larger entity.

A company must steer and control all its activities, which includes projects. The main element of company steering and control is the allocation and usage

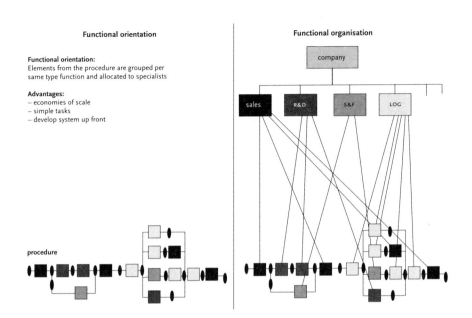

Functional orientation

Functional orientation:
Elements from the procedure are grouped per
same type function and allocated to specialists

Advantages:
– economies of scale
– simple tasks
– develop system up front

Functional organisation

company

sales   R&D   S&F   LOG

procedure

Figure 1.5 Functional orientation and functional organisation

of people, money, and other resources in order to effectively produce products
for its stakeholders. As this is so important, companies use a structure (pictured in a company's organisation chart) and a set of rules, regulations and
procedures. This set, and the people who have been allocated the task of controlling it, we call the bureaucracy. A good project manager adheres to the rules
of the bureaucracy because it increases the effectiveness of his project team.

Companies consolidate their organisations in order to reduce complexity and
to increase efficiency. Contemporary organisation structures focus predominantly on function, i.e. pre-defined parts of the structure have the responsibility to carry out specific functions for the entire company (see Figure 1.5).
Examples for such parts (these are called divisions or departments) are
Finance, for the financial functions, Manufacturing for producing the primary
manufacturing goods, ICT for information and communication technology,
and Personnel & Organisation services for human resources. All associates in
a company 'report' via the organisation structure. Budgets, facilities and
resources are allocated to and managed by the entities in the structure. Any
process requiring a specific functional task must proceed that task through the
part of the organisation that is responsible for the function.

This functional organisation structure (Gailbraith 1973) is based on maximal division of labour (Taylor, 1927; De Sitter, 1982; Van Amersfoort, 1992) and aims to predominantly increase the efficiency of repetitive (fixed) processes. It is less effective for incidental or one-off processes such as a project.

A project is an incident that disturbs the structure for repetitive processes. It is an incidental process that takes a place in the company for the duration of the project only. The people working on the project do not report via divisional or departmental lines but via project management structures.

In large companies, one often sees that a project connects to the normal structure via a steering group, an organ in the company in which several regular divisions and departments are represented (Figure 1.6). The steering group can exist for the duration of the project only, though sometimes companies maintain permanent steering groups for projects. The project manager reports to the steering group for his project team.

The main reasons for separating projects from the normal structure are:
I   *Focus and priority*. Practice shows that if a person combines responsibilities in a repetitive process with project work, then almost without exception, the repetitive process takes precedence over the project. By separating the

26

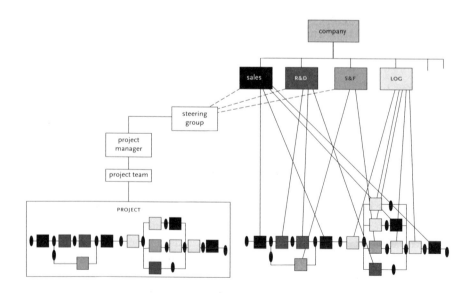

Figure 1.6 A project, a one-off process in a functional organisation

project from the repetitive processes, and by establishing an independent power structure for it, projects receive the required focus and priority.

2 *Inter-divisional/departmental process interfacing.* Interfacing is the execution of the coordination in a process. Interfacing takes place when work is distributed between parts of the company. In repetitive processes, the work breakdown is defined by the organisation structure. Finance plans and performs all the finance work, Sales all the sales work and so on. Repetition enables continuous improvement of the interfacing through learning from feedback and to improve for the next time. Consolidated interfaces (everything that is exchanged between activities) connect all the different activities together into the repetitive process.

In projects, there is no next time and no feedback. As the project will run only once, the work breakdown and the interfacing between the parts must be designed beforehand.

By severing projects from the normal structure of the organisation, their breakdown and planning become independent from the fixed organisation structure and can aim for the most effective split and the most effective interfaces. We shall handle interfacing in more detail in Chapter 3.

27

Research institutes and engineering offices sometimes hold functional organisation structures that accommodate projects better, e.g. with project-type or customer-type divisions. They can do so because their main process is to carry out projects, which are often rather standard and have an element of repetition. Please remember that we are still using 'company' as a representative for any type of larger entity. For your interpretation you may want to replace company with university, co-operation-agreement or institute or whatever more there is that constitutes the larger entity for your situation.

1.6 A project, like any process, must generate value

'Mission' is the most frequently occurring reason for the failure of projects (see Chapter 6).

The mission is the purpose of the project, the reason for existence. Remember our definitions given in Section 1.2:

- 'A project is a one-off, independent process with the objective of creating a predefined result.'

- 'A process is the named function for turning an agreement with a stakeholder into a delivered product and to receive a proper reward.'

The result of the project will be exchanged with stakeholders for a proper reward. There, proper means nothing less than: with a value profit for the company. If the mission is not right, in other words, if it can never bring a value profit, then the project will fail. If the product exchange with the stakeholder is not visible, then the mission is not visible. Therefore, in our terms, a process comprises a complete stakeholder process. If a project is only a part of a stakeholder process, then the project team does not communicate directly with a stakeholder but with the preceding and following project teams, and mistakes in communication can emerge and hide the mission (Figure 1.7).

The mistakes result from two main reasons:
1   the internal party relays the agreement wrongly to the stakeholder (the perception of the planned project outputs) (*wrong plan*).
2   the internal party relays the result wrongly to the stakeholder (the perception of the delivered project outputs) (*wrong result*).

The difference between the perceptions is caused by the fact that time has passed and that agreed anticipated products are replaced by real products.

The representatives of the company and the stakeholder who perform the task of selling, the negotiators, have the best perceptions of what is meant by the agreement. Not all of the agreement will be put on paper. Negotiators build a mutual understanding for the unwritten part that is based on trust. There are assumptions that result from their understanding of the agreement. Though

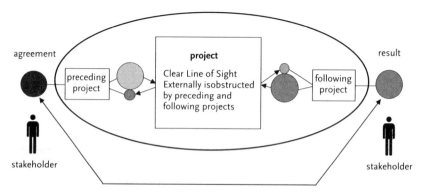

Figure 1.7 A project that covers only part of the stakeholder process

not set down on paper, if the assumptions are not met, neither stakeholder nor the company will be satisfied.

The assumed part of the agreement often contains elements that can change because the circumstances change. Very often the assumed part of an agreement entails secondary products that must accompany the primary products of the project. If a project team does not properly understand the value perceptions of the stakeholder, then they cannot properly understand the outputs they must produce and also cannot take advantage of the freedom of execution that is often present in secondary products. Project teams that do not negotiate directly with stakeholders receive relayed primary steering information for their projects. Indirect information increases the chances of taking the wrong decision. Therefore, if a project team has no direct links with the final stakeholders, then they should try as much as possible, to create such a link. They need insight into the eventual stakeholder and product exchange.

We call insight into the stakeholder exchange 'Clear Line Of Sight Externally' (CLOSE). This is pictured in the Business Effectiveness Loop (BEL) in Figure 1.8.

Project outputs, (the products), are exchanged for other products (the rewards). The value gain results from the values of the resources used in the project and the values of the rewards received. Value gain is profit expressed in all possible types of resources rather than only in money.

29

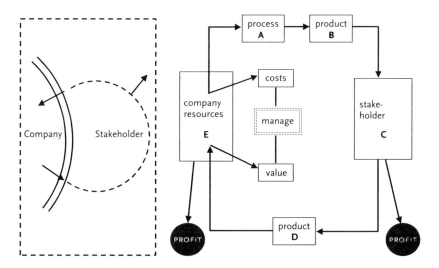

Figure 1.8 Business Effectiveness Loop

The business effectiveness loop circles between company and stakeholder. Company E deploys resources in process A to produce product B for stakeholder C who adds the product to his resources. Stakeholder C deploys resources to produce product D for company A who adds the product to its resources. Company A and stakeholder C perceive the value of the received product as higher than the value of the resources they deployed. CLOSE means a good understanding of the BEL for the project.

Example

Company E is a university, stakeholder C is a student. The university deploys resources such as teachers' time, knowledge and teaching skills, buildings, PCs, library. The process A entails e.g., lecturing, exams, practical exercises, and counselling. The product B entails e.g., lectures, information, exams, and diplomas. Stakeholder C is the student and the affected resources are, e.g., his knowledge and skills. Product B is delivered by the student to the university and comprises, e.g., money, loyalty and research outputs.

Often, a process produces secondary products in addition to primary ones. They are of many kinds and encompass information by-products, gained images, knowledge and skills acquired, etc. Sometimes the value exchange from secondary products outweighs that of the primary ones.

Example

In 1960, the US Government started a project with the primary product of 'putting a man on the moon and bringing him back to Earth safely'. The value of the primary product can be qualified (put in words) in terms such as a method for space transport, one kilogram of Moon dust, a worldwide boast of image and respect for the country, and the regaining of the number one position in the World in space science. Additional values were achieved in abundance, though, from the by-products of the process; think of energy cells, solar panels, oxygen recycling, heat resistant ceramic materials, free-fall moulding, etc. Products that have found markets outside of space travel. The combined values of these by-products nowadays dwarf those of the primary products.

Both value steering and the type of process must be taken into account while managing process effectiveness.

1.7 Design for effectiveness

The 'Improve' cycle presented in Figure 1.9, uses the business effectiveness loop to design effective processes. Design is counter-clockwise:

1 Develop a clear understanding of the stakeholder (C) receiving the products (B).
2 Develop a clear understanding of the products (B) and of the stakeholders' (C) perceptions of their values and value changes.
3 Develop a clear understanding of the process (A) that delivers the products (B) and of the flexibility needed to adjust the process to value changes.
4 Develop a clear understanding of the costs of the process (A), i.e. the value sacrificed because of the consumption of resources (E) by the process. Also, develop a clear understanding of the flexibility that is required to adjust the costs of process (A).
5 Develop the application flexibility of resources (E).
6 Develop the understanding of the products (D) required from (and returned by) the stakeholders (C), their value effects for the company and of how these can change.

Note that the steps do not need to start at point (1). They can start at any point. The design process must keep cycling until the anticipated result is satisfying.

31

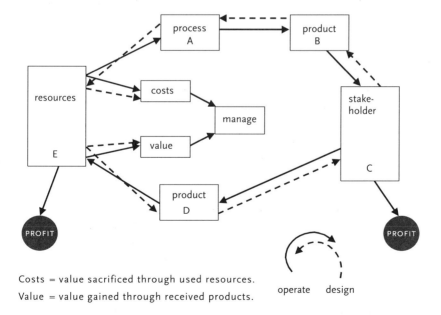

Costs = value sacrificed through used resources.
Value = value gained through received products.

operate   design

Figure 1.9 Process improve cycle

Example

The project to design and develop a new toy for children:

- *Step 1* is understanding the stakeholders. In this example, we restrict ourselves to one of the stakeholders: the consumer. It entails understanding the child as well as the parents and others who could give the toy as a present.
- *Step 2* is understanding the product that would merit the appreciation of children, their parents and others, and the secondary products that must accompany the primary product. They are, for instance, advertisement and product information. This step also means understanding the stability of that appreciation. Will it be a hype-product, only selling for a short period? Or will it be a product that will be there for a long time? This defines the required flexibility of the process that produces the product must be.
- *Step 3* is to define a process that is capable of delivering the product and that can also match the flexibility requirement. It could also entail comparing in-house manufacturing versus buying and co-manufacturing.
- *Step 4* is to understand the costs of such a process. That means to assemble a complete list of resources required, including hard resources such as money, materials, equipment, and labour as well as soft resources such as knowledge, skills, and information.
- *Step 5* is to develop the allocating capability of the required resources. If present knowledge does not suffice, it should be built up. If insufficient trained labour is available, then it should be acquired.
- *Step 6* is to develop an understanding of what is required in return from the stakeholder. That is not only money but also secondary rewards such as 'spreading the word about this wonderful toy', ideas about improvements and enhancements, loyalty, timely payment, correct behaviour, and also feedback and complaints.

Example

Design a way to measure radioactive contamination of the water in the Barents Sea. Again we shall look at the main stakeholder only.

Let us assume that an environment protection association (SeaSafe) initiates and funds the project. Step 1, understand the stakeholder entails, e.g., looking at SeaSafe more precisely. Seasafe's mission is 'to advance environmental safety and healthiness at sea'. SeaSafe's main means of operation is to search and detect real and potential dangers and to harness public opinion in order to force authorities to take corrective action.

Alternatively, let us assume that a nuclear power plant Dynamo Murmansk (DM), that takes cooling water from the Barents Sea, initiates and funds the project. Step 1, understanding the stakeholder now leads to a completely different picture. DM's mission is to provide for reliable, cheap, and safe energy to north-west Russia. dm's main concern is survival: to prove that their plant does not add radioactive contamination to the (possibly already contaminated) seawater.

Step 2, understand the products for the stakeholder and his perception of their values. SeaSafe wants to be alerted to any danger, including, e.g., that from sunken submarines, even if they are not leaking radioactive material, because they are a potential threat. DM will require proof of contamination upstream and downstream of their water intake and exhaust points. SeaSafe will require proof of contamination at any location in the Barents Sea. They will also require comprehensive information of sunken boats including such details as type of nuclear engine and fuel, nuclear warheads, other cargo, and pollution history.

Step 3, understanding (and in this case designing) a process that will produce the required products, follows directly from steps 1 and 2 and will differ quite a lot if for SeaSafe or for DM. So will steps 4 and 5, assess the costs and develop the flexibility of the required resources for the process.

Step 6 is the value of the rewards returned by SeaSafe or DM. The appreciation by the company that carries out the project differs because the image value of the customer differs. For example, a project carried out for SeaSafe will carry a higher image value than a project carried out for DM.

1.8 A project must fit within the context of the company

A project must fit within the context of the company and in the environment of the company. 'Company fit' is the extent to which the project connects with the company outlines. We distinguish the main company fit elements:
–   the restrictions the company set itself;
–   the company style and culture;
–   the company standards, norms and (shared) values;
–   the company rules and procedures;
–   the company infrastructures and systems.

Company restrictions exist simply because a company cannot excel in everything. Every company must focus on a limited range of products, markets, processes, and resources in which it can operate and excel.

Example

Recent history. In the late 1980's, when mergers became the dominating route for companies to grow in size and importance, many companies neglected their sets of constraints and restrictions. Incorporating merged-in staff into the base management structures inevitably followed the mergers which should produce the main financial benefits but also resulted in increased spread of attention and a consequent loss of focus. Companies encountered problems to keep up profitability due to increased complexity.

It led to a reaction movement which was called 'back to core business'; it meant that companies kept the elements that fit within the company restrictions and laid-off the rest. (Strangely, the obvious alternative was seldom observed; to put a number of highly independent and clear-focussed sub-companies in parallel under the umbrella of a predominantly financially focused consolidated company.)

Another example occurred with a company that installed bespoke software for supermarket counter systems. They were one of the first (and the best) to use the bar coded EAN[1] on packaged products. When they enhanced their product range with licensed software for connecting

---

1   EAN: European Article Number standard serves, amongst other things, for product bar coding.

> information systems, they were suddenly not seen any more as the best in a specialist' area but as a starter in the general software area. They lost their USP (Unique Selling Proposition) because they broadened their range of products and, as a consequence, changed from a highly profitable original software maker into a marginally operating software package installer.

Company style and culture originate from the styles and beliefs of the people who started the company and who may still be the owners. They often are of an ideological nature: To be honest operators, to be politically independent, to positively discriminate against minorities, to be seen as leading innovators, to allocate 25% of the profits to the development of local society, or to be self-sufficient financiers. But sometimes they are the personal owner's desires such as: to be bigger than the company that once fired him in the past. Company prerequisites impact the processes and projects in the company. They also impact the style, culture, standards, norms, and values of the company, the way that the associates behave, and the way they expect to be treated by the company.

Styles and cultures live very long lives. Even decades after becoming independent companies, previously nationalised institutions can still maintain a civil-servant style and culture.

The rules and procedures are effectuated in the company's bureaucratic system. Good bureaucracy is a blessing, not a burden. It facilitates correct application of necessary rules and procedures. A good project manager takes advantage of the bureaucracy.

Adhering to and making use of the bureaucracy saves the project manager a lot of time. Bow to the rule and go ahead instead of resisting it and spending days and nights getting simple decisions approved or taken. Never fight the bureaucracy at the cost of one's project.

The last element of outlines derives from the practical long-term commitments formed by the company's infrastructures and systems. Because these cannot change rapidly, processes and projects must connect to them.

> **Example**
>
> If a project must use computer equipment and software, then it better connect into the existing infrastructure and stick to existing offerings. Even if other products would be better, the interest of the company is not served with too great a variety of equipment and software.

1.9 Project mission, vision, and strategy

Mission, vision, and strategy can be defined for large elements such as the entire company as well as for such parts as one division or department, one process or one project. A lower level mission must fit in with, and is subordinate to, the higher-level mission.

The role of mission and vision is to clarify and agree direction of the company, department, or project and to create a consensus of how it must develop. It helps to make that clear to all relevant people and it helps in planning the efforts. In short, it helps to develop the strategy.

- The mission is the reason of existence, 'the purpose'.
- The vision describes a compelling picture of a future state when the mission is successfully achieved. A vision is an attractive aiming point. A vision is also a choice for a specific way *how* to fill in the mission.
- The strategy is the main line of planning to develop and achieve the mission.

Note that there are many different definitions in use for mission, vision, and strategy.

Vision brainstorms serve to choose a particular way of filling in a project mission such that it provides a clear point to aim at and fits within the available resources and time span. It is a high-level output-driven breakdown that also indicates which deliverables (outputs) will be produced first.

Project teams benefit greatly from a clear and well-understood project mission and a shared vision on the project. They provide one clear purpose and one attractive aiming point to all team members, hence to reduce the different interpretations in the team as well as between the team and the decision-takers, and they make a great start to developing a strategy of how to tackle the project.

Example

The mission is to have a good time in Amsterdam. The vision is a picture of us arriving in Amsterdam, well rested, ready for shopping, and maybe having a drink at a terrazzo on the Leidscheplein and watching the passers-by. The strategy is how we go to Amsterdam (by train of course, not by car) who we go with, who we will meet in Amsterdam, and how shall we contact her, by phone, fax, or other?

Please note that the vision is a choice. An alternative vision pictures us listening to the Concertgebouworkest in Amsterdam playing Mahler, having dinner afterwards and enjoying the company of good friends. The strategy entails the way we contact the friends, how we get tickets, how we shall make the trip, etc.

Example

Imagine a company that makes and sells shoes for very tall men. They have worded their mission as follows: our mission is to provide a complete, attractive, and high quality offering of footwear for men with shoe sizes 12 to 19.

Some environmental trends and changes, so the management assumes, will affect the business in the future. The main ones are:
- special shops for tall people continuously lose a market share;
- e-commerce gains a market share;
- average shoe sizes continue to increase steadily;
- Eastern European shoe manufacturers try to step into the market with cheap products.

The company has worded its vision as follows: in five years, very tall men will look for our brands first when they need shoes. Our brand name has become the top brand for expensive, high-quality, large-size footwear. With our innovative and fashionable collection we have won several times the recognition of the Dutch Society of Tall People and we have won similar and equivalent prizes abroad. Our market share of the footwear for tall men in Europe has grown yearly by 1 full point to 15 %, while at the same time, our brand image enables us to maintain an average 27% gross profit margin.

The strategy contains plans to maintain as far as possible the sales via special tall people shops. Further plans include building up an e-commerce facility and maintaining and extending the collection. Maybe there is a plan to sell sizes 12 to 14 shoes to normal shops, since there are more and more 'normal' people with these sizes. Maybe there is a plan to build up e-commerce together with a factory that produces large sizes of clothing or footwear for tall females. A flexible strategy will allow for keeping options open.

Example

The project is to produce this PPM course. The mission is to prepare students for future job situations so that they can contribute confidently and effectively when working on projects or managing project teams.

The PPM project team pictured a vision where students apply and enhance the skills that they were taught during the course. They regularly refer back to their study notes when planning and managing complicated projects and they keep on giving positive feedback to the university about how it helps them in their work. Their success rates are extremely high and their companies and institutes send their young managers away on PPM courses.

The mission and The rather ambitious vision focussed the team upon the valuable deliverables of the course and helped to define the main line of strategy. The team decided that 'confidently and effectively applying the skills' points to a course based upon learning through studying a comprehensive case in which students are invited to identify the problems by themselves and create their own solutions. Problem oriented learning: the lecturer feeds in theory, methods, and tools when there is already a need. It was decided to use one case that extends and develops during the course. That allowed the team to create a certain measure of complexity and to show a comprehensive picture of the problems and challenges of project planning and management. The team also chose group assignments in order to practise learning about projects.

Example

A project, funded by the UN for a village in Ethiopia.

The mission is to build an irrigation system and to donate it to the independent small farmers who use the water. The system must also continue to perform after the project has been terminated and it must remain in the ownership of the villagers.

The vision could be worded as follows: In 10 years, the village has become a role model for effective foreign-aid projects. After the initial project, the irrigation system has been extended and enhanced by the villagers themselves without any further help from outside parties. The decision procedure for water sharing is widely known and copied for its honesty and democratic design. The villagers have successfully defended their irrigation system against attempts to purchase it or to take it away from them by rich land owners.

In setting up a strategy for the irrigation, when focussing upon the vision one would opt for hiring the farmers to do the work and for making them use their current farming tools or tools that they will be able, and can afford, to use later. The design would include a democratic and honest water-sharing procedure that is linked to maintenance obligations and maybe also crop planning. The project would take great care to ensure that the property is well described and authorised and that all possible legal and moral steps to protect the property are taken. Possible future enhancements would be looked at and probably catered for, e.g., by oversized feeding channels. The design exercise would be made by a number of villagers (train them, produce the design together with them, and give them all the credit) with the objective of ensuring that sufficient skills and motivation are present in the village to make later changes and enhancements without outside help.

39

See also Campbell *et al.* (1990), Campbell and Tawadey, (1993), Hamel and Pralahad (1989).

1.10 Project development phases

In Chapter 7, we define a project as a series of six main development steps in time and we shall subdivide the steps further and go into the details. The split of the project we show here is by time sequence (Figure 1.10). In Chapter 3, we shall see that time sequence, or process-driven is one of three possible ways of splitting a project into smaller steps.

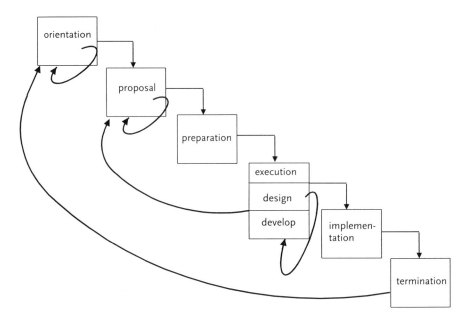

Figure 1.10 Overview of project steps. Process-driven project split up of 'any project'

With a range of sizes and complexity as large as what we understand under projects, any overview can only give a summary of what could be done and of a good sequence of doing it. The project team and its manager must choose what is relevant for their project and to what depth the steps should be executed.

Also the duration of a project phase varies according to the project. With research projects, one often sees that they begin and end using few people and proceed slowly, while the main phase involves many people and proceeds quickly. Investment projects start slowly, the decision to go on being postponed many times, but once it is taken the project must proceed as quickly as possible.

1.11 Project complexity

Project complexity is directly related to project costs and chances of failure. If a project becomes complicated, it becomes increasingly more expensive and its chances of success are reduced. If we turn it around, we can say: 'If it is possible to reduce a project's complexity, then the costs to complete it will reduce and the chances for a successful completion will increase.'

Reduced complexity works out in lower costs and fewer chances of mistakes. Some elements of complexity cannot be influenced. Other elements can and it is worth our while to do so. Let us look into a number of elements of complexity.

Project complexity depends not only upon the contents but also upon the environment of the project, the size and complexity of the project team, and the size and complexity of the customers. The same project can work out different for different companies, for instance, because internal systems and procedures that are easy and slick in one company are cumbersome and sticky in another.

Interference between project functions affects complexity. If more interference is possible, then more effort must be put into thinking the interference through and into the design of the solutions. Interference can be influenced with clever interfacing. Split points between parts of the project's functions that need only slow and easy-to-understand interfacing between them reduce complexity (see also section 3.6).

The number of receivers of project outputs affect complexity, not only because more people have more wishes and more people must be consulted and trained, but also because more managers must be consulted and be involved in the decision-taking.

The size of the project team affects complexity. The larger the team, the more time-consuming it becomes to keep everybody well informed. Every person added to a team doubles the time required for in-team communication. The positive part of size is the potential of team synergy. The negative part is the time required for communication. It all depends upon the project, of course, but in general, in groups of four the positive effects still outweigh the negative. When a team becomes as large as six, it is better split into subgroups. When a project team grows above 16, it may need a two-level management hierarchy, e.g. a project manager and two supervisors.

Highly specialised persons and a large variety of disciplines can increase team complexity and make it necessary to split in smaller subgroups even more quickly. The split points should be chosen in such a way that the interfacing between the parts is slow and simple. Do not split a project into parts if the activities in these different parts are subordinate to each other or if the information that the subgroups must exchange is difficult to understand. The objective for the split, to reduce the need for communication, will then not be achieved.

Splitting a project up into subgroups reduces the potential for synergy and learning but if team members rotate through the subgroups, some of the loss can be regained.

In a simple project, most of the costs and efforts go into development (see Figure 1.11). When a project becomes more complicated, more efforts should be put into preparation and design. The reasoning is simple:
– More chances exist to make mistakes in a complicated project.
– The earlier a mistake is recognised, the cheaper it is to cure (in a complicated project more efforts must be made to prevent mistakes).

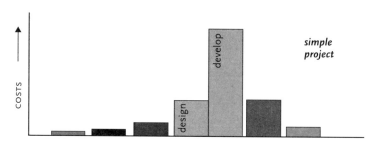

Figure 1.11 Relative costs per project phase. Project complexity affects the relative importance of the development phases of a project.

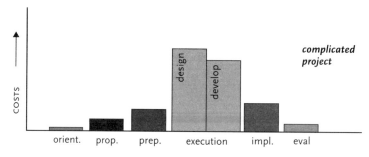

Figure 1.12 Effect of insufficient preparation

A mistake that is discovered during design is relative cheap to correct; no further effort is required. Correcting mistakes becomes more expensive when the project evolves, e.g., when the mistake is discovered during implementation. Neglecting this observation has cost many projects dearly.

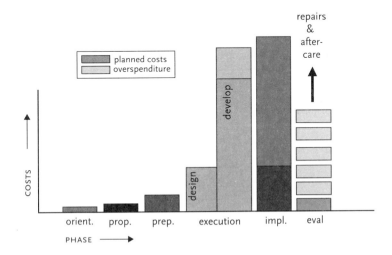

Figure 1.13 Effect of insufficient preparation and design for a complicated project

Figure 1.13 shows planned and actual costs of the phases of a project to install one standard ordering system replacing 15 national systems for a big international company. The size and complexity of this project was greatly underestimated and, consequently, insufficient effort had been planned for preparation and design. The underestimation resulted from the misconception that a reputed standard package would succeed in removing national differences where previous attempts for unification had failed.

2 Project Management

Learning objectives

The purpose of this chapter is to clarify the purpose of project management and to explain ways of managing a project effectively. After reading it, the reader will understand what is expected of a project manager and of the interaction with his team. He will understand the importance of timely agreeing honest criteria, adequate mandates, and effective liaison procedures to link the project with the rest of the company. He will understand people-, quality-, and resource-management. He will have gained an understanding of Self-Regulating-Teams, a potentially highly effective way of team cooperation.

This chapter contains explanations of responsibility, liaison, quality, and people within the context of projects. Different leadership styles are open to a project manager. They are explained together with the corresponding styles of team members. Projects use resources in order to produce desired project outputs. Project management involves resource-value management. Resource-value is sacrificed because of the consumption of resources and gained because of received rewards. Resource-value is also gained because of in-project learning. The project team can gain valuable knowledge and skills while working on the project.

Project management entails the management of
1. responsibilities;
2. liaison (connecting a project with the company);
3. quality; and
4. people.

2.1 Responsibilities

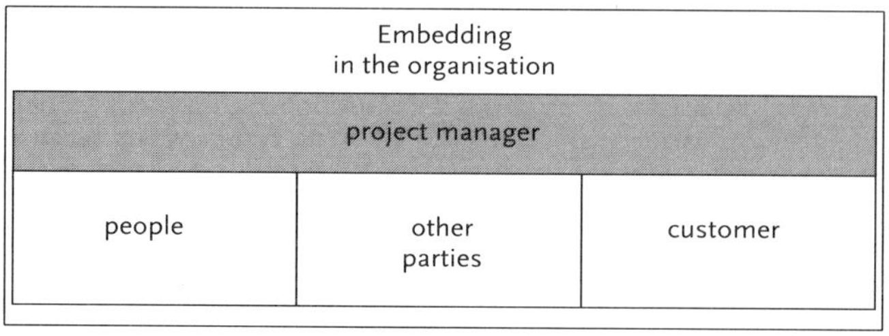

Figure 2.1 Embedding in the organisation

Responsibility is the essential manifestation point for a project manager (Figure 2.1). He is seen to be responsible for a successful delivery of project outputs, for the success of the project for the owners, for the optimal application of the project team, and for effective co-operation with other parties. He is the bridge bearing the project train. At the same time, he must live in a situation where he is not the only bearer of power. He must negotiate on behalf of his project. Even then, decisions for the project may sometimes be taken outside the realm of the project manager. For instance, a project can be cancelled when company interest has diverted from project objectives.

The project manager is not the only link with the main receiver of project outputs, the project's customer who may have concurrent projects with the same company. He may double as a supplier to the company and even as a supplier for the same project. The project manager must be aware of other links and, if he can, he must support and facilitate them.

Other parties will exercise their powers in the project. Think of the Personnel Department that retains responsibility for recruiting or firing people or the Buying Department that keeps control over approving or disapproving suppliers. Often, the project manager must share his power over the team members with the departments that they originate from and will return to after the project.

A project manager's responsibility is to produce the required project results within time, quality, and resource constraints. Hence the project manager is responsible for everything. But on the other hand, he does not hold all the power. This all puts the project manager in a tricky position. He must negotiate with others in power and he must compete with managers of other projects and processes for company resources. Please understand that this is not necessarily a bad situation. A complex company stays sound through not giving too much power to any one person. The sensible project manager anticipates this situation by agreeing a responsibility and control matrix with other parties. An example is shown in Table 2.1.

Table 2.1 The responsibility matrix clarifies the roles of the project team and other departments of the company

Responsibility and control matrix	Project team	R&D	P&O	Finance	Buying	Director
Proposal	D	R		R		A
Design the survey	D	A				
Costs calculations	D	R		A	R	
Benefits calculations	D	R		A		
Detailed plan for the survey	D		R			
Execute the survey	D					
Process the survey	D					
Reporting	D	A				
Evaluate	R	D				A
Send out invoice	A			D		

D = Do, R = Review, A = Approve
The responsibility matrix clarifies the roles for project team and other departments of the company

A good project manager ensures fairness and protection for the project against events and circumstances that are outside his control and that can disrupt the project (Figure 2.2). Make no mistake, guilty or not, if a project fails, some of the failure will rub off on the project manager and his team.

The project manager must define the borders of the responsibility. He must anticipate damaging events, not minding the source they may come from. He must try to prevent them and if he can't, he must report them as early as possible, demanding that they are removed before they hit the project and he must not be afraid to stop the project if they aren't.

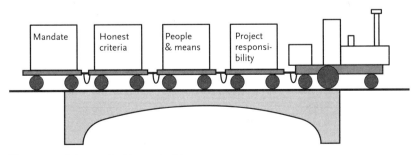

Figure 2.2 Fairness for the project team

A project manager takes a risk for the company. He undertakes something that has never been done before, it could fail.

2.2 Project liaison

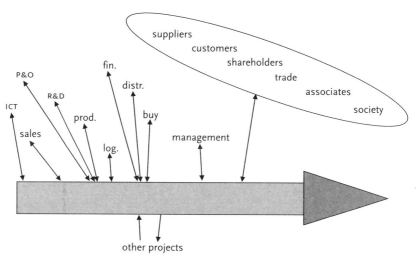

Figure 2.3 Project liaison

The project manager is the spokesman for his team and the main communication channel between the team and the rest of the company, other projects, and the stakeholders.

It does not mean that all communication must be actually handled by him; indeed it is often more efficient when the team members communicate directly with the outside, but he must take into account that, for the outside world, he is the first connecting point. He must be aware of the entire liaison for the project.

Liaison is the embedding of the project in the company. It encompasses the co-ordination of the communication and responsibilities with other departments and other projects in the company, with company steering powers, and with parties outside the company. In short, all the necessary interfacing between the project and the outside world. The project manager holds different mandates for his liaison outside the project. There are three main liaison lines:

1 *Liaison with other departments and other projects.* This liaison concerns project inputs, outputs, and facilities that must be exchanged with regular departments and other projects. The liaison activity must be scheduled

equally to any project team activity, even though the team will not execute the activity itself. Indeed, the project depends upon the correct delivery of input or take-off of output. The project manager must have a sufficient mandate to act for the project such that conflicts and the involvement of higher powers are avoided as much as possible.

Example: The P&O Department must provide working facilities such as a room, desks, and computers for the project team.

Example: An implementation project must approve and take responsibility for output produced in a preceding project.

2   *Liaison with the management team or steering committee responsible for the project.* Subjects here are progress, budgets and costs, cash positions, reviews and occurrences that require action but are outside the project manager's mandate.

3   *Liaison with suppliers and other outside parties.* Subjects are inputs, outputs and facilities that must be exchanged with external parties. This liaison is similar to that with other departments, though the project manager has a different mandate and, in the case of conflict, must initiate other procedures and involve other powers.

Example: A supplier of project equipment or a software house that must produce a computer system. The project manager must consult with the Buying Department when dealing with the supplier. On the other hand, Buying must consult with the project manager for project-specific dealings with a supplier.

49

2.3 Quality

Quality is measured on the scale of good and bad. Quality criteria describe the measurable aspects of good. Quality means many things of which the most prominent are reliability, safety, usefulness, aesthetics, and predictability. Quality in a project addresses many items, amongst which the most prominent one is project output quality (quality of the products).

Quality management means ensuring that the project outputs meet the quality standards set out for them. One reason more for singling out quality comes from the observation that often quality interpretations are not only held by the targeted stakeholder but also by the steering group and company management, company departments, other project teams, and last but not least, the members of the project team. With so many parties holding their own interpretations of quality, there is a real danger of mismatches.

At the end of the proposal phase (see the overview in Section 7.1), the quality interpretations of the stakeholders and the company representatives are fine-tuned and put into output specifications and quality measuring criteria. These are essential inputs for the design of the outputs. They become important parts of the agreement and must be part of the project proposal, though sometimes this is not yet possible in which case the proposal describes an agreement to further specify them in the design phase.

Example

Quality criteria describe quality in measurable terms. Examples: the quality of new production equipment could contain criteria for uptime, time to repair, and incident frequency. The quality of fruits could contain water percentages, size limitations, colour ranges (with spectra or sample cards) and deterioration (e.g. percentage that still qualifies good after x time under given conditions). Quality criteria can and must be designed at an early stage of any project. Sometimes it is not easy. E.g., which quality criteria can you think of for a survey of European citizens towards the permissibility of kosher slaughtering, or for the development of a stochastic model for forecasting rainfall in Monrovia?

An example of a project that failed because of mismatching quality assumptions:

An institute for water management assigned an engineering firm to develop a stochastic model of water withdrawal in the Veluwe (a national park in the centre of The Netherlands). The model should serve to enable conclusions and recommendations as to how much fresh water could be withdrawn from the area without endangering the park's ecologic system.

The firm developed a model that enabled conclusions with an accuracy of 90 %. In order to realise this degree of accuracy, the institute could even save on the current costs of soundings, which the firm claimed as an additional benefit for its model. The firm's engineers considered 90% 'a better than normal' accuracy for this type of model. The institute for water management refused to pay for the model because they had assumed a far more precise model, with an accurate of 97.5% or better.

If quality criteria had been agreed up front, relating to accuracy and the numbers of soundings, the difference in accuracy assumptions would have easily been avoided. The firm's engineers would have discovered that one particular threat to the park's ecologic system was responsible.

'Not to lower the groundwater below the penetration level of polluted external water.' The institute's engineers considered a 10 % uncertainty in the matter of drinking water pollution unacceptable.

Quality management in a project means also ensuring that company quality standards are met for the working performance of the team, e.g. for planning and progress management, for associate guidance and appraisal, for budget control and cash management, for information and reporting, and for project representation. For some, some of these company-wide criteria may be available. For others, they must be agreed between the project manager, the team, and the other parties involved in the particular element.

Example

An example of where a project manager omitted to make such an agreement: A Dutch software engineering firm produced a small computer system for the Dutch subsidiary of a large international company. Within two months, the system was produced, documented, and installed, the people were trained, and all was running correctly and smoothly. The users were very pleased, and so was the Dutch management.

CICT, the international's common global information and communication technology service company, had set the global standards for all software produced externally. Amongst other things, it contained a standard quality assurance report, a comprehensive document (>100 pages) that catered for all possible quality elements of systems development projects. The Dutch software engineers had produced their own quality report, which, technically, was completely satisfactory. CICT, though, refused to approve payment until a standard quality assurance protocol (QAP) was completed. The software firm argued that a standard report was unnecessary and would involve putting many irrelevant facts to paper. It was all in vain and eventually they had to produce a QAP. It cost them an additional two months to understand the questions, to look up data that was of no consequence for this project, and to answer more than 1000 seemingly irrelevant questions. The firm made a loss on the project.

CICT was right! They were the appointed guardians of systems quality and the qap was their means of control. That the qap was very inefficient for this small project was, in their judgement, of little consequence. The QAP provided them with a standard means of control that served all systems,

51

including the most complicated ones, which was an advantage that far outweighed the extra costs for small systems.

The project manager had wrongly assumed that his way of working and his quality interpretation would be satisfactory to the customer.

2.4 People

In this section, attention is paid to modern views of how humans work effectively together. Many of these views stem from modern SocioTechniques (Van Amersfoort, 1992; Emery and Trist, 1965; De Sitter, 1982).

People management is one of the most important tasks of the project manager. People management must be aimed at many goals at the same time of which the most important ones are:

1   To ensure that the team members' outputs stay in line with (possibly changing) stakeholder demands by facilitating their understanding of these demands *(Clear Line Of Sight Externally (CLOSE))*.
2   To ensure effective communication and co-operation in the group and to accomplish a high level of group synergy (group synergy, extraordinary results achieved through close interaction between people).
3   To develop the team members' capabilities and capacities through combining *Doing, Learning, and Coaching (DLC)*.
4   And, last but not least, to ensure that the team members feel happy, free and secure and, at the same time, challenged and motivated to perform an excellent job in an excellent project.

The attentive reader will observe that the very functions of traditional people management, planning, work distribution, and output control, do not appear in the above list.

The modern people manager tries to shift as much as possible of the traditional management work to his team and the individual members of the team. This goes beyond delegation, which is more or less a temporal shift of mandate, means, and responsibility.

In the preceding sections we have pictured the management and liaison task for a project predominantly as representation and enabling. The remaining task for the team and its members is mainly focussed upon producing the project's outputs.

It has been proved many times that teams can plan, distribute, and control their own work very well. Nevertheless, the manager carries the responsibility, especially in the view of everyone outside the project. Inside the project however, manager, team, and team members perform the planning, work-distribution, and output-control tasks in a dynamically complementary way. If the team lacks the capability, then the manager will step in and do the task while, at the same time, he will train his team. The team will regulate itself and team members will operate in an entrepreneurial way.

Of course, self-regulation, can only be effective in a team with sufficient insight into the project and sufficient drive and sense of co-operation. The insight in the project we call Clear Line Of Sight (CLOS). In entails understanding what the project is about, the means, the targets, the planning, what must be achieved, and how it will be achieved. The insight to the results of the project we call Clear Line Of Sight Externally (CLOSE). Externally points to the importance of the value exchange with the outside, with the stakeholders. CLOSE is a prerequisite for associate entrepreneurship (to act as if one works for one's own company), which can open new roads to considerable improvements of effectiveness.

A lack of CLOSE existed in the example of the water withdrawal model (see Section 2.3).

Though known for a long time in factory processes, Self-Regulating Teams (SRTS), or autonomous work groups, are rather new for information and knowledge workers. A limited number of pilots have shown promising advantages:
1 Very high learning results are possible.
2 Individuals' needs to control their own work are provided for in a flexible way hence increasing chances for happy and motivated associates (Loeffen 1999) (the most important factor is: improved desired capacity/given capacity to influence own work).
3 A number of reasons for tension and stress are removed.
4 Improved production per associate (pilots 20 – 50 %).
5 Team members will understand the synchronisation and interfacing better and therefore reduce the risk of mistakes and failure.

Another hard lesson was learned with the pilots: SRTS will most likely fail if management is not prepared to relax control. A team is not self-regulating if its manager still wants to know all the details and influence all decisions. An SRT requires facilitation rather than management old style. The facilitating manag-

53

er sees his task as an enabler and synthesizer (to make a whole out of elements) for his team to perform.

A facilitating manager serves his team rather than that the team serves their manager.

2.5 Leadership styles, management styles

There are many views on leadership styles some of which are summarized below. The last styles (5 and 6) describe a SocioTechnical view.

1   *Manage*. The boss plans and organises the work and the necessary facilities and provisions. He leads the workers while they perform their tasks and he controls their outputs. He takes responsibility for the whole and ensures that the workers have all the facilities and means for their allotted tasks. This style is rather protective for the worker.

2   *Tell*. The boss tells what the worker must do and controls what he has done. There is not much 'leadership' in this style. It leaves no freedom for the worker. The boss has total control though still makes the worker greatly responsible; if something is not good enough, in his exclusive judgement, then he takes corrective action, to his exclusive judgement. It even gets worse when the boss also tells the worker how he must do the work. The tell style provides for many opportunities to make the worker unhappy.

3   *Delegate*. The boss delegates a task to the worker. He provides for the necessary means and leaves some freedom for the worker although keeping some control in his own hands. Sometimes the boss delegates a responsibility; the worker must take action on the boss's behalf. Depending on the details this style can work quite well but there are many ways to delegate wrongly.

4   *Lead*. The boss leads the worker by setting the goals and providing for the means to achieve them. This leadership style leaves much freedom and initiative to the worker, though in a protected way. The leader-boss knows intuitively how much control he must keep in his own hands. Good leadership is a preferred style for many workers but unfortunately natural leaders are very rare.

5   *Facilitate*. The boss takes care to see that everything around the worker is all right and allows the worker to define the goals and to achieve them in, as much as possible, an independent way. He leaves as much as possible control to the worker. This style makes the worker highly self-sufficient, which often fits him well but sometimes leaves him rather lost.

6   *SRT*. Self-Regulating Team. The team directs itself to achieve company, team

and individual goals. The 'manager' of a self-regulating team creates conditions and the stimulation for the team to operate as if the team members had run their own enterprise. He is also the visual representative for the team. This *SocioTechnical* style ensures that optimal advantage is taken of the qualities and talents present in a team and it creates the conditions for an extraordinary team performance. Most workers function well in a SRT, but a few loners just cannot work in a team.

Take care, though, as there are confusing circular referencing definitions around, e.g. to lead is a subtask of to manage and to manage is a subtask of to lead.

Abbreviation memory aid

Manage	POLC	Plan, Organise, Lead, Control
Tell	PC	Plan, Control
Delegate	EC	Empower, Control
Lead	SMITH	Steer, Motivate, Initiate, Train and Hoover
Facilitate	E	Enable
SRT	FAE	Facilitate Associate Entrepreneurship (SocioTechnical view)

55

Example

A plan-control style manager for a self-regulating team accumulates conflict upon conflict. Two teams were trained to become SRTat the same time. One team was responsible for a very complicated repetitive process. A man whose responsibilities were widespread managed this team. He had little time to spare and he also had the courage to change his style of management and relax control. His team very quickly became a role model SRT and, after a short while, achieved great benefits for company and team. Mistakes went from 100 a week down to almost zero, team production went up with 20 %, plus it took up several new tasks. Examples of added tasks: to redesign the process (more flexible), to make a process guide, to give training to external suppliers, and to reorganise their process filing such that it became generally accessible. That was not the end; the improving never actually stopped.

The other team was also responsible for a rather complicated repetitive process that needed to interface closely with the aforementioned team. Their manager felt very uncertain if he was not abreast of all details and he could not let loose. After a frustrating period of attempts to become more self-regulating and a series of misunderstandings and conflicts,

> manager and team reverted to the old tell and control style and they did
> not achieve improvements. Although the team members started out very
> enthusiastically, they did not become self-regulating. Also, this manager
> had widespread responsibilities and little time to carry them out but he
> could not bring himself to trust his team. Rather, he worked 80 hours per
> week controlling them. He also did not want to change because his own
> superior evaluated him in a very controlling style.

Conversions to SRT are more a manager's change than a change for the team
members.
Self-regulating in projects is potentially even more advantageous than in repetitive processes. Indeed, in a project, all steering is based upon observation and
anticipation, a task that is better performed by the entire team rather than by
the manager alone.

2.6 Resources

The costs of a project are not only the money spent and material and facilities
used, they consist of all resources consumed by the project. Resources are all
the company possessions. Often they are called assets, though most companies
comprehend assets as being only a subset of their resources.

Resource management refers to using and generating company resources in
the most effective way. That counts for all the processes, including the projects.
Effective means generating new value in a most efficient way. Resources originate from the bartering between the company and its stakeholders. The obvious resources are money, labour, equipment, and stocks. But knowledge is a
company resource as well and so are information, image, brands, products,
shape, etc. A very important, but often ignored resource is shape: the capability
of people to work together. In a smoothly running company, there is a mutual
understanding of how things are done, people have elaborate communication
networks, and they know each other personally. It costs a lot of efforts to build
that up again if it were lost. A very important resource too is options: what
could be done and would return a profit, but is not actually done at the current
point in time? Options are often accidental, sometimes very valuable by-products
of projects. In project teams, people from different parts of the organisation
and different disciplines come together; a unique forum for breakout ideas. A
new option can change the value of other resources.

Example

'There are too many people (too much labour).' can be rephrased as:
'There are not enough options available'. Removing the excess labour
(firing people) means losing their knowledge and skill values. A new way
to utilise the labour increases its value and nothing is lost!

Table 2.2 Types of resources

Abstract ←					TYPES OF RESOURCES → Concrete
					Half-products
			Systems	Data	Money
		Knowledge	Processes	Facilities	Materials
Ideas	Image	Markets	Recipes	Procedures	Technical materials
Options	Relations	Brands	Skills	Information	Raw materials
		Alliances	Shape/attitude	Licences	Labour
			Infrastructures	Products	Finished goods
					Equipment

Resources are of many different kinds. They can be concrete and abstract, finite
and infinite, and have many different characteristics. One could envisage them
as layers feeding and being fed by processes. Time affects the resource values, as
does allocating, or giving away, the resources. But different resources react differently to time and allocation. Look at the Figures 2.4 and 2.5 for examples.

57

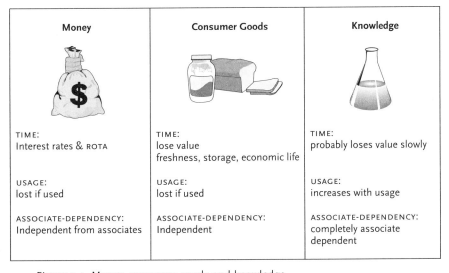

Money	Consumer Goods	Knowledge
TIME: Interest rates & ROTA	TIME: lose value freshness, storage, economic life	TIME: probably loses value slowly
USAGE: lost if used	USAGE: lost if used	USAGE: increases with usage
ASSOCIATE-DEPENDENCY: Independent from associates	ASSOCIATE-DEPENDENCY: Independent	ASSOCIATE-DEPENDENCY: completely associate dependent

Figure 2.4 Money, consumer goods and knowledge

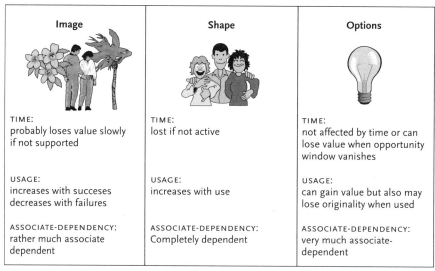

Image	Shape	Options
TIME: probably loses value slowly if not supported	TIME: lost if not active	TIME: not affected by time or can lose value when opportunity window vanishes
USAGE: increases with successes decreases with failures	USAGE: increases with use	USAGE: can gain value but also may lose originality when used
ASSOCIATE-DEPENDENCY: rather much associate dependent	ASSOCIATE-DEPENDENCY: Completely dependent	ASSOCIATE-DEPENDENCY: very much associate-dependent

Figure 2.5 Image, shape and options

People are the bearers of many company resources of which knowledge is the most obvious one. Knowledge is a strange resource. It can be consumed without losing it and even gains value when it is used. But knowledge is only one step in a chain from data (facts) to applied knowledge. Value is only created when knowledge is applied. For instance, to design a solution, to take a decision, or to perform an activity. Knowledge that is never applied has no value for the company.

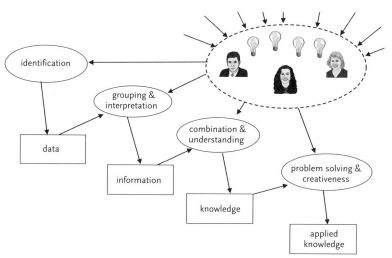

Figure 2.6 The human addition

Data are facts such as invoice details, customer addresses, and product properties. The bulk of company data is nowadays commonly recorded in databases.

Information is interpretation, aggregation, and combination of data such as turnover, available stock, and product profitability.

Knowledge is the understanding of information within a context and supporting it with structures and thinking models. Profitability information combined with what he sees and feels 'in the field' helps a marketer to understand the market. It helps him to learn and build up his experience.

Applied knowledge is being able to use knowledge. The marketer can apply his knowledge together with his experience, structures and methods, and his creativity to direct and adjust his actions for the best result.

In Figure 2.6, traditional learning moves from left to right: it starts with interpreting and combining data (facts) into information and continues with generating knowledge by combining and understanding information. The team member must still learn to apply the knowledge. In self-regulating teams, do-learn-coach (DLC) learning moves from right to left; the team member already understands the problem and solves it right away, guided and aided by his colleagues. The knowledge and the supporting information and data he will find easily because he already understands its role.

2.7 Social responsibility

The project team and its manager must demonstrate 'socially responsible behaviour'. Not only does this mean that team members behave correctly, it sometimes means that they must cope with ethical problems. What if the team discovers violations of company rules? What if a supplier offers bribes? What if a team member pursues his personal interests at the costs of the company's? What if a fraud at another company is discovered, e.g. at a customer or a supplier? Practise proves that project teams do encounter such problems and must cope with them.

These situations involve applying judgement, weighing interests, and assessing consequences in order to choose the best or the least damaging approach. Weighing and judgement means criteria against norms and standards and these do not come from one uniform set. They are not the same everywhere, e.g. a gift for a professor is good behaviour in one country while it is corruption in another. Work on Sunday, eat pork, kill a cow, etc., are against the rule in some religions. Some companies apply one world-wide set of company rules while other companies follow the mainstream in each country.

Although there is no simple uniform answer, the following weighing process is rather applicable in most situations.

Step 1   What are the consequences, what is the best approach, for the company, and for the project in particular?

Step 2   How do I, as an individual, think about it, referring to my personal norms and standards and what is the best approach for me?

Step 3   Am I, or otherwise who is, the right person to make the judgement for the company and the project and who must take responsibility for any measures necessary?

3 Planning

Learning objectives

The purpose of this chapter is to explain methods, techniques, and tools for effective project planning with special emphasis on approaches to project breakdown. After reading this chapter, the reader will have learned how to split a project into manageable parts and how to design efficient interfaces between them, interfaces that reduce complexity without creating much extra work. He will know and understand planning jargon, such as work breakdown, sequential and parallel running, critical paths, milestones, expediting or crashing etc. He will also understand the necessity of the planning of the interfacing and liaison with outside parties. The reader will have learned the principles of how to design a flexible project plan that leaves openings for opportunities when they present themselves and can cope with obstacles. Further, he will understand the outlines of using spreadsheets for project-planning.

This chapter discusses structures, methods, techniques, and tools for effective project decomposition and planning, including process-, output-, and skill-driven work breakdown, estimation of costs and duration, expediting (speeding up) or crashing a plan, and the use of milestones. Different types of interfacing and their consequences are explained in detail. The chapter ends with an IDEF (Information DEFinition) model for the design and continuous updating and improving of a project plan.

3.1 Work breakdown

Almost every project, but certainly large and complicated ones, must be broken down into smaller parts. If done well, the complexity of the project is reduced, the broken down (small) parts are easier to allocate to team members and the project will become more manageable. See Figure 3.1 for understanding the hierarchical representation of a project breakdown.

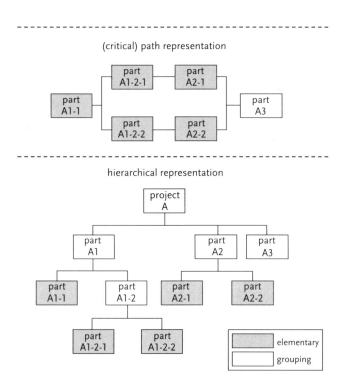

Figure 3.1 Breakdown of a project

Another representation technique is 'network' which shows the execution sequence of the parts of a project. Network is often used in critical path planning systems (see Appendix 2, Figure 2.2).

There are three main entries for breaking down a project into parts:

1   Contents or output-driven;
2   Activity or process-driven;
3   Function or skill-driven.

Bertrand, *et al.* distinguish between (1) product structure, (2) manufacturing steps, and (3) capacity available.

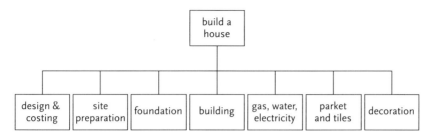

Figure 3.2 Process work breakdown.
Building a house subdivided into process steps. This subdivision says much about the main steps but nothing about the house itself. For instance, building a school would be exactly the same. It also says little about the type of work and the skills of the person doing it.

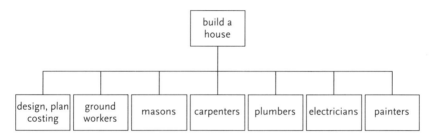

Figure 3.3 Functional work breakdown.
Building a house subdivided into functions or skills. This breakdown also would be equally valid for a school as for a house. A project broker could make a plan like this. It shows the parts in the same way as he can contract them out to specialist subcontractors.

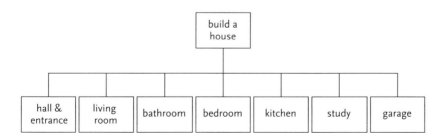

Figure 3.4 Contents work breakdown.
Building a house subdivided into contents or outputs. This breakdown says everything about the house but nothing about the sequence activities or of the skills needed. In Asia, it is quite common to build a kitchen and a bedroom first and to add the other parts gradually, when needed and when money is available. This is also known as component breakdown.

A realistic project plan will show elements of each of the three breakdowns.

See Figure 3.5 for how the high-level (process-driven) breakdown is further subdivided. Any of the parts can be subdivided further in any of the three entries, output-, activity-, or skill-driven.

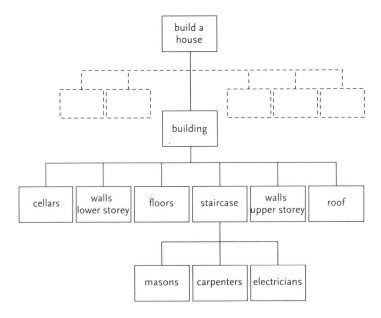

Figure 3.5 Work breakdown

Example

For a project to do a survey of citizens' satisfaction of municipal services, a breakdown could be as follows: (1) counter services; (2) police; (3) education; and (4) outdoor services.

1   Counter services could be broken up again into
1.1   civil;
1.2   administration;
1.3   unemployment aid;
1.4   taxes;
1.5   city planning; and
1.6   housing and construction.

2	Police could be broken down into
2.1	traffic;
2.2	crime;
2.3	security;
2.4	administration of foreign citizens.
3	Education could be broken up into
3.1	schools;
3.2	library; and
3.3	redeployment;
3.3.1	redeployment courses for obsolete industry worker and
3.3.2	for physically handicapped persons.
4	Outdoor services into
4.1	waste;
4.2	roads;
4.3	plants and park.

This is a contents or output-driven breakdown. The parts represent subsets of the future output of the survey.

On the other hand, we could break it down as follows:
1   to specify the objectives and the scope of the survey;
2   to acquire the funding for the project;
3   to design the survey processes;
4   to carry out trial surveys;
5   to improve the design with the findings from the trials;
6   to prepare for the execution of the survey;
7   to carry out the surveys;
8   to analyse the outcome;
9   to compile a detailed report;
10 to make a management summary; and
11 to publish the outputs.

This is an activity- or process-driven breakdown of the project. The parts represent subsets of the sequence of activities of the project.

Skill-driven would look like:
1   all the statistical work together;
2   all the financial work together;
3   all the police expertise work together;
4   all the traffic work together;
5   and so on.

Work is put together on basis of the skills required to execute it.

Contents, component or output-driven breakdown defines the structure of the output parts but not necessarily the sequence of building the parts, while the process- or activity-driven breakdown generally defines that sequence. Indeed, one cannot publish the end report before the surveys are analysed. Skill-driven leaves all the sequence problems unsolved, and even increases them, but sometimes cannot be avoided, e.g. legal activities will probably be taken out and given to the lawyers. With some highly routine processes, skill-driven breakdown is given first priority order to facilitate the out-sourcing to specialist firms. For instance, a project developer would split a project to build 50 houses into subprojects for specialist building firms, e.g. (1) ground preparation, (2) foundation, (3) masonry, (4) carpentry, (5) electricity, (6) decorating.

1   Output-driven first priority enables selecting the highest value parts for earliest delivery. Output-driven also presents ways of reducing risk of project failure, e.g. if there is an output part upon which the success of the total project depends, then it is best to do that part as early as possible. Alternatively, place independent difficult outputs late in the project in order not to delay the other outputs if they take more time or fail. It also covers selecting the outputs for the easiest recipients first, e.g. for a cabling company to lay new cables in the most densely populated parts of the city first.

2   Process-driven first priority enables combining process steps in order to gain economies of integration, since all the outputs are in the same process step at the same time. It is also the easiest for putting activities into a sequence (planning).

3   Skill-driven first priority enables economies of scale through the concentration of similar types of work. It becomes more possible with routine, e.g. a series of similar projects.

There is no easy general answer for the question of which type of breakdown must have first priority. Every project is a new challenge to take advantage of specific project opportunities and to reduce specific project risks. Consequently, for a good project work breakdown, one needs not only information about the type of work, the required efforts, the needed facilities, and resources but also the mutual dependencies, the receiving stakeholders, the potential benefits, and the risks.

If, for instance, in a project, many different outputs are completely independent from each other, then the execution sequence can be designed for early value delivery. (A project specific property defines the best breakdown.) On the other hand, if one very expensive machine must be hired for the independent outputs, then the execution sequence can be designed to concentrate all the usage of that machine into one as-short-as-possible period of time. (Again, a project-specific property defines the best breakdown.)

Each type of breakdown has its own advantages and disadvantages. For a very complicated project, it is advised to avoid a skill-driven breakdown because it makes the project inflexible and very difficult to control. A process-driven breakdown would make the project easier to plan but would deliver no value (no products) until the very end of the project. If this value is important and an early output-driven breakdown would be possible, then that should be seriously considered. Output-driven breakdown requires careful and sometimes difficult interface design at an early stage but it enables a build-up of results together with costs, hence reducing cash requirement.

Summarizing: with some caution, one could state that generally the best first priority breakdown is:
– output-driven for risky and complicated projects;
– process-driven for high interference projects; and
– skill-driven for routine projects.

Example

In our example survey of citizens' satisfaction of municipal services, this could work out in different ways. Imagine that the city council has become very concerned about safety and security. They urgently need the citizens' views and observations. As this is the perception of the requester and funds provider of the survey, it means that the value of the police survey is higher than the value of other surveys. That is a good reason to do the police service survey first (output-driven). On the other hand, if there is a perception of bad services but it is not clear what the problems are, then it is better to execute sampling surveys in all areas first (process-driven).

Activities and their interfaces

Planning must show detailed activities in a sequence. We can rephrase this as follows: planning must show intermediate outputs in a sequence. Intermediate outputs are interfaces between activities.

The design of every individual element of a work breakdown consists of selecting an activity and designing the interface(s) to connect the activity with the rest. There is a choice here: to start with designing the activities and to accept the resulting interfaces or to design the interfaces and to accept the resulting activities. Current practice shows that almost invariably activities are designed first, which is a pity because often it is far more effective to design the interfaces first and to accept the resulting activities.

3.2 Estimate duration, efforts, and costs

After having broken down the project into sufficiently detailed parts, the efforts they require, their durations, and their costs must be estimated. The most likely types of costs of a project will be covered in the following list although there may be projects with other costs:
– costs of materials (e.g. raw materials);
– costs of location (e.g. office rental);
– costs of services (e.g. secretarial);
– costs of systems, tools and equipment (e.g. payroll system, machine running costs);
– costs of consumables (e.g. printing paper for the office);
– costs of energy (e.g. electricity);
– costs of stores and warehousing (e.g. storage and manipulation of goods);
– costs of leases and licences (e.g. the use of a patents);
– costs of subcontracting, (e.g. a part of the project is out-sourced as a turnkey project);
– financing costs (e.g. interest of loans);[1]
– man- or man-time-related costs which include: total-worth salary costs, costs of travel and accommodation, costs of training.

Man- or man-time-related costs are often not easy to determine. It is so difficult to make accurate man-time estimates because in a project, a lot will happen for the first time. There is no feedback from previous occurrences. Remember, a project is a one-off process. Even if a project is very similar to a previous one, there can be differences in the circumstances of the project that make them incomparable. Other reasons for differences can derive from the composition and the experience of the team, the interference by management, the weather, the location, the suppliers, new products and tools, etc.

---

1 Financing costs are often not the domain of the project manager but of the corporate cash manager. E.g. the decision to buy or lease will be taken by the cash manager and the financial consequences of that decision are the cash manager's responsibility and do not show as costs (or benefits) on the project C&B.

Experienced project managers refer to their own and their colleagues' previous projects and judge using available insight and their gut feeling. Software development companies and engineering firms often use comprehensive systems and tables to estimate the efforts for types of work that have an element of repetition (programming per function point, ground clearing per m^3, painting per m^2, laying cabling per m.)

The best advice for project managers is to build their own reference base. Use the plans and actuals of previous projects. Even better is to coordinate this with other project managers. It is a good idea to review a project plan together with a couple of experienced project managers.

Take care, in theory, one person is available for 261 days in one year. Practice shows that information workers deliver no more than 200 production days per year and often even considerably less.

Table 3.1 Example of the losses

8	general holidays
28	individual holidays
8	absence through illness
5	divisional/departmental obligations
1	company obligations and festivities
7	training
4	miscellaneous
61	total

Project managers and supervisors must count with even less productive days. They 'lose' more time on company and divisional obligations and they must perform people management tasks. Rule of thumb: 25 days per year for every report.

Sometimes, the absolute duration of an activity takes priority over all other. Take, for instance, an office move. It must be completed in one specific weekend when equipment is disconnected, furniture is taken out, walls are painted, and cables changed, after which the furniture and equipment is brought back in again, installed in new places, and connected. Electricians, carpet layers, and several other outside parties have been hired for this specific weekend. If the work takes more effort than foreseen, one can only add more people and work overtime because slipping into Monday morning would play havoc and is just not open for discussion. In this example, the start, the end, and the duration are all fixed and efforts and costs are subordinate.

Absolute timing for activities can derive from calendar items: A Christmas promotion project in The Netherlands must take place between December 6 and December 24 (after Saint Nicolas Day and before Santa Claus).

Sometimes costs take priority and duration is subordinate. Take the example of a project that must deliver a new process-training manual. If the department has no budget to pay for extra manpower, then it can decide to have the manual produced by the process operators when they have time to spare. In this example, the costs are fixed (at zero extra man costs) and the duration is subordinate.

The activity 'transport a new bulldozer from Baltimore to Rotterdam by boat' has fixed costs and duration while there is hardly any (project team) effort required.

Often it is wise to estimate ranges (best and worst cases) and to design a plan that can flexibly cope with drawbacks and opportunities.

Effort required to perform an activity can vary a lot depending on the person who carries it out. The most common reasons for this are in the properties of the person. Do not underestimate this. For system development (programming) and construction engineering, performance differences can be as much as 10 to 1. The experience, skills, talents, energy, intelligence, and perseverance of the person must match the demands and complexity of the activity. This match will affect the quality of output and the duration of the activity. If the activity is too difficult, the person may never finish it. But there are also activities that are little affected by the person. Think of surveillance or attending a conference.

In a large project with a certain amount of uncertainty, it is important to choose the detail and depth of breakdown carefully. The near future should be broken down into much detail because the detail will be required soon. But the distant future should not be broken down too deeply. There is too much risk that something will happen and make the detailed plan invalid (see Figure 3.6).

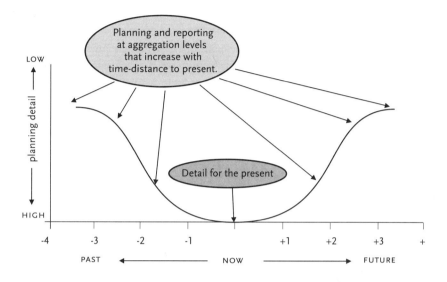

Figure 3.6 Reduce vulnerability to change

Take care to provide for good tools and working situations. They can also affect the duration of activities considerably. Good communication facilities can speed up activities.

71

Example

A secretarial service has been found to improve the effectiveness of a project many times.

Every project team member works with information and creates information. He produces files on paper and on server disks. Much of this information is worked on and used by other team members. Practice shows that multiple copies of the same information being changed by many people cause mistakes and doubles the amount of work. A secretary can file and structure the filing for the entire project team and prevent mistakes and double work.

3.3 Critical Path[2]

Figure 3.7 depicts a project of five activities. The arrows represent the mandatory sequence between the activities. (The pointing activity is a precedent of the pointed-to activity.) There are two paths in the plan because activities B and C can run in parallel with activity D. The longest one of the two paths is the critical path.

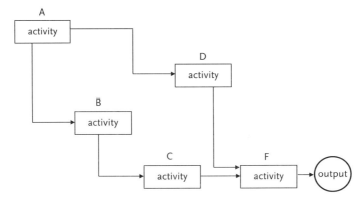

Figure 3.7 Work breakdown structure

Figure 3.8 shows a Program Evaluation & Review Technique chart (PERT). The critical path is printed in red. It is a good indicator for the project manager to decide where to place attention in order to expedite the project. PERT was developed by U.S. Navy in cooperation with Booz-Hamilton and the Lockheed Corporation for the Polaris missile/submarine project in 1958 (Baker and Eris, 1964; Dean, 1985; Naik, 1984).

In the example of Figure 3.8, the upper path is critical because the sum of the duration of the activities (6 + 17 + 9 = 32) is more than the sum of the duration of the activities in the lower path (6 + 6 + 6 + 9 = 27).

Figure 3.9 shows how activity D can be split into two activities, D1 and D2, that can run in parallel. Now the duration of D (17) is shortened to the longest one of D1 (11) and D2 (6). The path duration is therefore reduced from 32 to 26. Now the lower path (A-B-C-F = 6 + 6 + 6 + 9 = 27) has become the longest and therefore is now the critical path.

---

2   The Critical Path Method (CPM) was developed by DuPont Inc. in 1958.

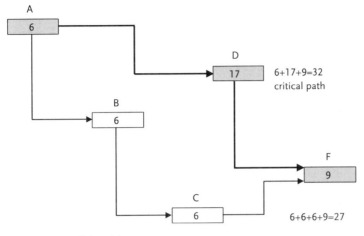

Figure 3.8 Work breakdown structure

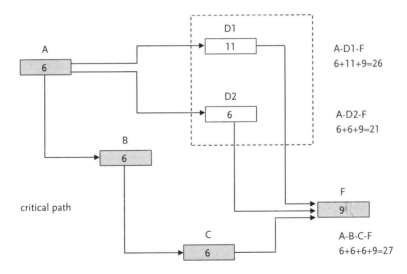

Figure 3.9 Work breakdown structure

Any shortening of duration of an activity in the critical path shortens the duration of the entire project. Any shortening of an activity that is not in the critical path has no effect on the duration of the entire project.

3.4 Expediting or crashing

Expediting or crashing is the term for reducing the duration of an activity. Activity D in Figure 3.9 was expedited by splitting it up into D1 and D2, which run in parallel. Figure 3.10 shows a further crashing of activity D by splitting it in seven parts, four of which can run in parallel.

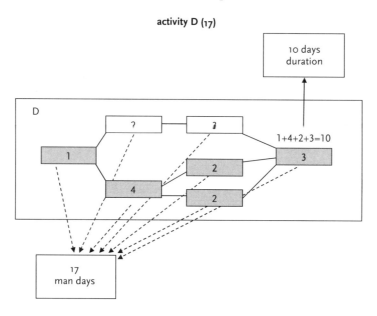

Figure 3.10 Work breakdown structure in parallel

Duration and efforts are two different properties of an activity. In Figure 3.11, the activity (D) requires 17 man-days of effort but, depending on how the activity is split up and executed, the duration varies between 17 and 8 days.

The duration of an activity can also depend on external factors. In Figure 3.12, it is shown that although the activity (to buy and install a piece of equipment) only requires five man-days of effort, the duration is nine days. The cause is the delivery time of the equipment, which is longer than the three days of preparation that runs in parallel with the delivery.

When activities can run in parallel, emphasis on expediting goes to the longest path. Activities in the shorter paths provide for freedom, e.g. to even out effort required over time. In Figure 3.13, the freedom to start with the five days activity is 10 days.

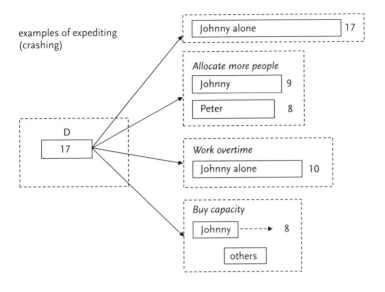

examples of expediting
(crashing)

Figure 3.11 Work breakdown structure

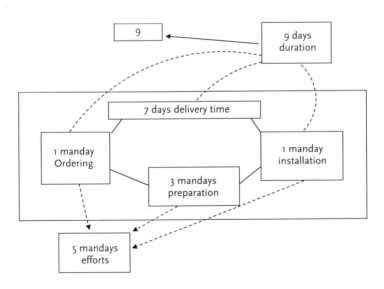

Figure 3.12 Work breakdown structure, external cause for duration

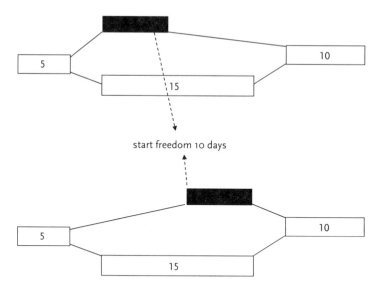

Figure 3.13 Work breakdown structure, smoothing and levelling

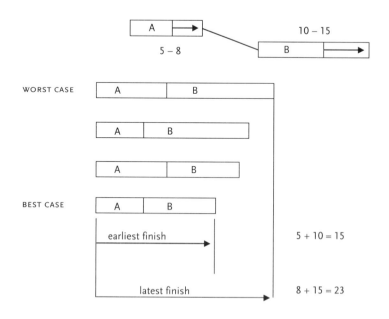

Figure 3.14 Work breakdown structure

Sometimes it is unclear how long an activity will take and a range can only be estimated.

As shown in Figure 3.14., the duration of activity A can vary between five and eight and that of activity B between 10 and 15. Activity A must precede activity B. The best case for completion of A and B is the sum of the shortest durations (5 + 10 = 15). The worst case is the sum of the longest durations (8 + 15 = 23). If the estimations are right, then the actual finish will be between the earliest and latest planned finish.

3.5 Milestones

Milestones are zero-duration activities that serve for improving the insight into the plan and for easier control. They are the traffic lights in a plan. If the light is green the next set of activities can begin, if it is red, it cannot.

Often a milestone is formalised in a document such as the minutes of a decision-taking meeting. If not so, however, it is good practice to include a formal document and to certify project progress with it. The milestone document must contain the completion criteria for the preceding phase and the checks against them.

Milestones, if chosen well, coincide with good interfaces in the same sense as we discussed in the previous sections and will explain further in the next section (3.6). Good interfaces cause little extra work, are easy to understand, and they are slow.

> Example milestones: approval of a drawing, the decision to proceed, a purchase order sent out, the receipt of materials, confirmation of availability, a document completed with all required information for a next activity, confirmation that the preceding, parallel activities have been completed, confirmation that budgets have been allocated, a point in time when there is a clear transfer to another procedure (load ship (ready to depart), ship departure).

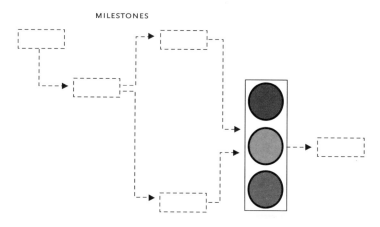

Figure 3.15 Work breakdown structure

Milestones are good review points for a steering group. The project manager can make use of them by carefully explaining to the steering group what freedom for decisions is present at each milestone. It clarifies implicitly the importance of the decisions they are asked to take.

78

3.6 Interfacing

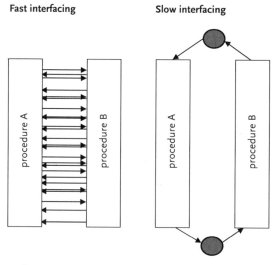

Figure 3.16 Interfacing

In Section 3.1 about work breakdown, we argued that it is almost always better to design split points and interfaces (connectors between the split parts) first and accept the resulting activities, than to do the reverse.

Good split points cause little or no extra work, the interfacing between the split parts is easy to understand and capture, and they are slow, meaning that they do not require frequent exchanges and/or communication. If a project is split up in such a way, then the total possible interference is reduced. If there is less to reckon with, then the project becomes easier to understand and chances of making mistakes are reduced.

Example

From the example of the municipal services survey (see Section 3.1), let us take the counter service survey as an example. One could split it up into specialist areas such as statistics, communication, crime, traffic, and create tasks for the specialists in these areas (skill-driven work breakdown). With such a split, there is the additional task of ensuring that the specialists' outputs will fit together. They will have to communicate very often with each other because the project outputs require contributions from almost all of them. The resulting interfacing will be complicated and frequent and so will create the need for extra efforts. The chances to make mistakes will be many. The advantages of the skill-driven break down would be the consistency and efficiency of the specialist solutions. On the other hand, one could take the outputs from an independent survey as a first-level subdivision and then split further into a logical sequence of required intermediate outputs such as:

1   scope and objectives report;
2   survey contents specification;
3   survey process specification;
4   survey materials;
5   output reports;
6   output analysis report;
7   conclusions and recommendations.

All these are easy to understand and slow, and will therefore be efficient interfaces. The inputs and outputs for the activities prescribe exactly what must be produced, thereby giving the people who carry out the activities a clear focus point.

The possible disadvantage of this output-driven work breakdown is that the consistency of the survey may be lost. Functional specialists would have to communicate in order to maintain consistency. This would however, be greatly facilitated if the specialists have a clear sight of the required outputs and their recipients (CLOSE).

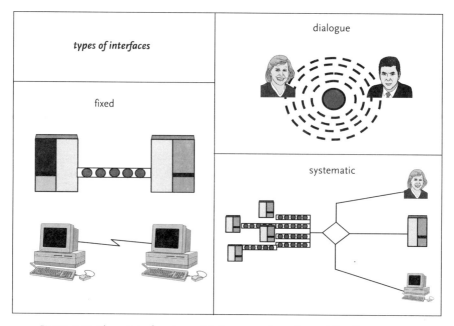

Figure 3.17 Three interface types (dialogue, systematic, and fixed)

In most cases, it will be possible to define a fixed interface to connect the parts at a split point. For instance, between the design and the construction of a house, the interface will include the drawing, the listing of materials, and the costs. Fixed interfaces do not leave elements open to interpretation or later choice.

Some interfaces can be left open, e.g. the choice of the equipment in the built-in kitchen can be made later. Depending on a later choice, one of the three of four prepared and calculated plans will be executed. This would qualify as a systematic interface. There is more than one option to choose from and the intervention of people is required to activate one of them.

In other situations, it may be neither possible to define a fixed nor a systematic interface at a split point. Assume that it is unclear what the owner wants to do with a part of the house. He will decide later and may choose to give it a common type of function or even may invent a new function for it. In such a case, it is best to plan a dialogue interface. The owner and the builder agree to hold a dialogue at an appropriate point in time in order to decide how to proceed. At that time, and not earlier, they will agree the specifications and the costs (dialogue interface).

Please think a moment longer about the above examples. Although a kitchen consists of real objects such as furniture, equipment, lighting, extractor fans, and needs real connections for water, gas, and electricity, real floors and real walls, the interfaces we use in the plan consist only of information. When the kitchen is actually installed, all the hard 'interfacing' must be available, e.g. the microwave can only be connected if the electricity and extractor fans are prepared, the kitchen can only be installed after the tiles have been laid. But the teams that must provide for the objects can plan and design their work already with the information about the objects they do not need the hard objects.

The interfaces needed to plan the link between parts of a project consist of information.

The best type of interface depends upon the situation. Look at the consequences of a wrong choice:

- If a fixed interface was chosen and later something changes, such that the interface does not fit anymore, then the connected activities must be done again.
- If a systematic or dialogue interface had been chosen, then redoing the activities could be avoided. A systematic interface in fact means that a number of alternatives have been prepared. Efforts have been made to cater for any possible changes. The more expensive flexible solution is traded off against the risk of having to redo connected activities.
- A dialogue interface means that knowledgeable persons interpret output from the sending activity in order to adjust it to the needs of the receiving activity. A dialogue interface costs efforts at the point in time that the activities must connect.

Interfaces must be as slow as possible 'without losing benefits'. If subgroups in a project need to communicate with each other several times a day in order to align their activities, then they start to behave like one big activity for one group, which increases complexity and, therefore, costs and chances of making mistakes. Without losing benefits means that the functionality of the total must remain intact.

3.7 The initial plan

The previous sections have handled: project breakdown into activities, interfacing between activities, execution sequence of activities, activities that can run in parallel, absolute timing of activities, and costs, required efforts, and duration. Now we have all the information available and can begin to design a good project plan. 'Good' is defined differently for different projects and circumstances but, in general, the objectives of a project plan contain the following elements:
– Fastest delivery of high-value generating outputs;
– Lowest project costs;
– Fastest completion;
– Smoothest deployment of labour and scarce resources;
– Flexible, capable of coping with change;
– Lowest risk;
– Highest support from relevant outside parties;
– Highest commitment of project team member.s

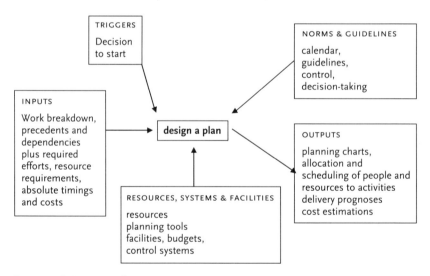

Figure 3.18 Design a plan

'Good' in technical terms means that the planning procedures and tools are easy and efficient in use. The iterative process of designing a plan is pictured in Figure 3.18. The basic exercise is to allocate activities to team members (or outside parties) and to time them while taking into account the capacities and restrictions of people and resources, and parallel or precedent relations.

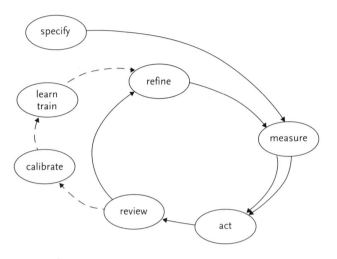

Figure 3.19 Continuous improvement cycle. (From SMARCT by John Thomson, GPR Consultants Ltd & Ron Asher, Mars Inc.)

A project is a one-off process. Feedback from previous identical projects is not available. But though real iteration is not possible, imaginary iteration is. A plan can be designed and changed and redesigned many times (see Figure 3.19) before it is activated. It can be improved until it is as good as imaginarily

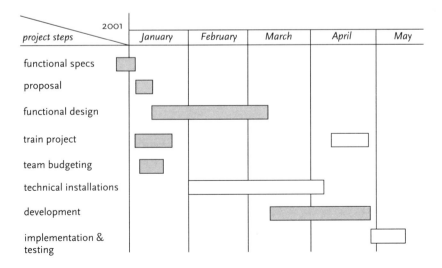

Figure 3.20 Gantt Chart

possible. And with every cycle through the planning process, the planners learn more, understand the project better and, consequently, plan better.

An activity plan is best pictured in a rows-and-columns sheet such as a Gantt chart (devised by Henry L. Gantt in around 1917) or in a critical-path overview. Figure 3.20 pictures a simple Gantt chart, showing time periods as columns and project steps as rows, e.g. the step functional specifications is planned in the last week of 2000 and the first week of 2001.

PERT charts show the mandatory sequences of activities and emphasise the longest duration path (critical path) (See Section 3.3. and also appendix 2).

Calendars identify time periods and allocate properties to them. Example: the days of the week, type of day, and the working hours per day (see Table 3.2).

Table 3.2 Working day calendar

Day	Mon.	Tues.	Wed.	Thurs.	Fri.	Sat.	Sun.	Mon.	Tues.	Wed.	Thurs.	Fri.	Sat.	Sun.
Date	16-1	17-1	18-1	19-1	20-1	21-1	22-1	23-1	24-1	25-1	26-1	27-1	28-1	29-1
Type	work	work	work	work	holiday	wknd	wknd	work	work	work	work	work	wknd	wknd
Hours	8	8	8	8	0	0	0	8	8	8	8	8	0	0

Working hours per day

In Table 3.3, the contents of Table 3.2 are grouped per week while working hours are now presented as working days.

Table 3.3 Weekly working days

Weeknr	03	04
Working days	4	5
Non-working days	3	2

Available capacity can be shown as in Table 3.4. It is a combination of a general working days calendar and the personal working day calendars of project team members.

Table 3.4 Project team availibility

Week No.	1	2	3	4	5	6	7	8	9	10	11	12	13	14	15	16	17	18	19
Alice	4	5	4	5	5	5	5	2		6	6	6	6	6	5	5		4	5
John	4	5	4	5	3	5	5	2		5	5	5	5	5	5	5	5	5	5
Peter	4	5	4	5	5	5	5	5		5	5	5	5	5	5	5	5	5	5
Lucille	4	5	4	5	5	5	5	5		6	6	6	6	5	5	5	2	5	5
Total	16	20	16	20	18	20	20	14	0	22	22	22	22	21	20	20	12	19	20

Available capacity in person-days

Individual calendars can vary from general calendars. In Table 3.4, Alice shows a six days per week capacity in weeks 10 to 14 because she plans to work on Saturdays and, in week 17, she plans to take a holiday.

Planning software

The planning tools currently on the market present a rich variety of planning functions amongst which are WYSIWYG[3], critical path, and optimising functions. Further, they provide a variety of ways to enter data and to retrieve information. Most software tools serve a specific purpose and are interfaced with other software for that specific purpose, e.g., computer aided design software. Take care, functions that fall outside the basic offering of the software can be cumbersome and time-costly. Most software products include costs and budgeting facilities. (See Appendix 2 for examples)

Many project managers, though, decide to keep activity planning separate from cost and budget planning and use, for instance, spreadsheets for the latter. The consequence is some extra data entries but it is far less complicated to operate two independent systems and, more important, to change them than one integrated system.

Spreadsheets (see Appendix 10) have features that are suitable for most of the required planning functions. The project team may have to invest time in learning some of the more esoteric spreadsheet formulas and macros but the advantage is that the planning tool can be tailored to the problem. Take care; the project planner/manager must plan and manage and not spend all his time programming rich and all-encompassing planning macros. If these are required, it is better to use a well suited planning package.

---

3   What You See Is What You Get. Changes are immediately effectuated in output presentation.

Resource requirement plan, costs, and cash estimations and delivery prognoses are plan derivates. They provide input to the plan and need the plan as input. If the plan must be changed frequently in the course of the project, then the derivates must be changed as well. In such a case, an integrated system that covers both plan and derivates can then be of advantage.

Table 3.5 A simple planning spreadsheet: manually allocates the remaining capacity to unscheduled activities.

	capacity		week numbers						total allocated	un-scheduled
	in (wo)man days		12	13	14	15	16	17		
		available	10	8	15	15	15	15	78	
activity	required									
orientation	12		4	8					12	0
proposal	2		2						2	0
design	34		4		15	15			34	0
build	18								0	18
deliver	3								0	3
total	69		10	8	15	15	0	0	48	21
remaining capacity			0	0	0	0	15	15	30	

See Appendix 10 for more sophisticated spreadsheets.

3.8 Keeping the plan up to date

The plan for a project must be frequently adjusted. Maintaining and improving it serves exactly the same objectives as the design but the process is triggered by real, as well as anticipated facts rather than by anticipated ones alone (Figure3.21).

The outputs not only show a plan for the future but also the facts of the past. The triggers contain such running facts as activity completions, relevant events, new and changed decisions, and detailed and/or revised work breakdown. The inputs contain actuals such as costs, people-time usage, usage of other facilities and resources, further activity completions, revised estimations, and capacities. Near-future activities are detailed out. Practise teaches us that most project plans are updated frequently (>once per week).

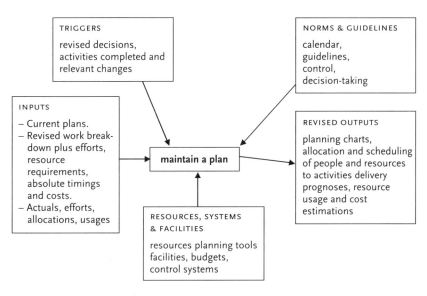

Figure 3.21 Maintain a plan

Planners build information on their own planning accuracy and on how much that improves by regular revisions, by keeping track of the original plan, plan revisions, and of actual completions (Figure 3.22).

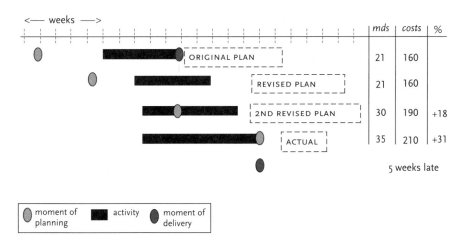

Figure 3.22 Keeping track of planning accuracy

4 Monitoring and Control

Learning objectives

This chapter explains projects from the point of view of running a process in a company. Like any process, it must be monitored and controlled. After reading it, the reader will have an understanding how to keep track of the resources used by a project and of the consequent costs incurred. He will understand the main resource usage terms such as planned, actual-to-date, estimate-to-complete, revised plan, and variance. He will also understand the importance of budget control alongside cash management and will have knowledge of ways to build flexibility into the cash timing of projects. Further he will understand the function of monitoring quality and of executing timely quality control.

The chapter contains information on structure, methods and tools for the monitoring and control of people's time and the use of resources. There are also sections on cash planning and quality monitoring and control.

4.1 People time and the use of other company resources

Monitoring and control of the use of resource provides information that is needed to keep costs and the progress of a project on track. It also provides essential input to keep the project plan and its derivates, such as budgets and cash plan, up-to-date and to provide essential input for progress reporting.

As people-time is one of the most important uses of resources, project team members must record time spent on a project, with a sufficient degree of detail, e.g. by person, by activity and by time period.

Some salary systems provide for transactions that enable recording associates' time and costs to project budgets. If the budgets can be as refined as far as to individual activities, then the system can provide all the input needed for project control. But take care with accepting control restrictions because of the limitations of a salary system.

Alternatively, the company may have a mandatory project control system (PCS) that accepts transactions of resource usage including people-time usage which interfaces with budget control systems. Some software packages provide integrated PCS, budget control, and salary systems.

Usage administration for the project is possible by using a spreadsheet. It is important to keep a check on the total time booked on projects with other systems, such as budget, PCS, or salary systems.

People time is best registered in a system that caters for frequent and efficient entry of transactions and updates. For instance, if people carry out more than one activity concurrently, it is not a good idea to register time spent only once a week. At the end of the week, people do not remember exactly how much time they have spent on individual activities. Either use pre-printed forms that are filled in each day, or at every change of activity, or provide for a simple system that does the same.

It is advised to preprint all planned activities per person per week so that entries need only contain hours spent and exceptions from the plan.

Example

The example booking form presented in Table 4.1, shows police survey activities of the citizens' satisfaction project and, particularly, the bookings of project team member Kees de Lange in week 12. This form is filled in every day and shows the activities that Kees is likely to work on in the current and near-future weeks, plus the hours already spent on the same project in previous weeks. The form is printed out by the project registration system and, when filled in, becomes input for the same system. Of course, this example could very easily be automated. Generally accessible spreadsheets on a network server are also well suited for teams of limited sizes.

Table 4.1 Project time registration form

					Wk 12				**hours**	

Name: *Kees de Lange*
Project: Citizens satisfaction survey
Subproject: Police Department (PD)

Activity	Sub-activity	Remarks	Planned hours	Act-to-date	Mon.	Tues.	Wed.	Thurs.	Fri.	Total week
Design survey	Design questionnaire	finished	8	12						
	Set up statistical model	finished	12	12						
	Sample with 10 persons	finished	20	8						
	Finalise	finished	8	4						
Send out questionnaires	Select representative sample	finished	16	4	8	8				16
	Addresses- envelopes	*fin*	16				8			8
	Send out	*fin*	4					*3*		*3*
Retrieve questionnaires	Book returned questionnaires		8							
	Send out reminders		16							
	Enter in stat. model		24							
Report survey	Analysis		40							
	Conclusions		24							
Interviews	Select 8 persons at PD	*fin*	2					*1*		*1*
	Prepare interviews		8					*4*	*2*	*6*
	8 interviews		64							
	Analysis		24							
	Conclusions		24							
	Select 4 PD's in other cities	*fin*	4						*2*	*2*
	Prepare interviews		8							
	4 interviews		32							
	Analysis		24							
	Conclusions		24							
Project management										
Project administration									*2*	*2*
Other	Other project									
	General meetings								*2*	*2*
	Courses & education									
	Illness									
	Holidays					*8*	*8*	*8*	*8*	*8*	*40*

Italics filled in by Kees de Lange

4.2 Cost management

During the project, actual costs must be booked at the time of incurrence against the planned costs. Costs result from people-time usage, as we saw in Section 4.1, and further from actions such as a purchase (e.g. to buy a computer), a contract (e.g. to hire an external consultant), or a cross-charge (e.g. for the use of secretarial services).

Some resource usages and costs are triggered and booked a the period of time (e.g. monthly rental of building) but more often they are booked by event (the receipt of a cross-charge or an invoice).

Sometimes, costs of resource usage are first booked to general accounts and only later syndicated or cross-charged to the accounts of the users (projects) of the services. The reason for this is often that only one company-wide invoice for the usage is received (e.g. energy bill). Sometimes, however, a company wants to keep a tight control on a usage of a certain type (e.g. legal advice, taxis, air travel, or telephone).

The project manager needs to plan all the costs he expects for his project per time period in which he expects them. In general, a costs plan is sufficiently accurate if summarised per month, though it should be set up per week if accurate cash planning is required.

The cost report shows detailed cost management information; planned costs, actual-to-date costs, estimate-to-go costs, revised planned costs, and variances versus planned costs.

A good automated project control system (PCS) will help with this though it does not require great effort to write a spreadsheet for a purpose that is inter-linked with people costs (see Appendix 10, spreadsheets).

Project-cost information is the basis for budget and cash management but remember, a budget serves for the authorisation to make costs, a cash plan serves to manage credit positions, and a costs (and benefits) plan serves to manage profitability.

4.3 Budget and cash management

The budget shows the planning of the costs of a project during the time period they will be incurred. The cash plan shows the total cash flow for the project in the exact periods that the cash is actually transferred.

Table 4.2 Example budget overview

	May	June	July	Aug.	Sept.	Oct.	Nov.	Dec.	TOT
Team costs	20000	16000	12000	16000	16000	8000	16000	16000	120000
Travel & stay	8000		4000			4000		6000	22000
Admin costs		8000	8000	24000	24000	8000	8000	8000	88000
Purchase equipment						415000	5000	6000	426000
Maint							1500	1500	3000
Consul						3000	2000	3000	8000
Comms								12000	12000
Rental equip							500	500	1000
Totals	28000	24000	24000	40000	40000	438000	33000	53000	680000

Team costs and administration costs are department-to-department cross-charges and therefore do not affect the cash position of the company. Actual payment agreements of cash-outs do affect the cash positions in the months they are planned for.

Example

Let us take the example of secretarial support for a project. It is a real cost incurred by the project and must therefore be included in a cost & benefit (C&B) overview. If the support comes from a general service department and is already accounted and budgeted for, then the project needs no reservation in its budget. But if the general service department does not have its own budget and must cross-charge the costs, then reservations must be made in project budgets.

No real cash will leave the company as a result of giving secretarial support to the project. Indeed, the general service is already paid for. Consequently, there is no need to update the cash plan of the company (assuming, of course, that no secretaries would be fired if there was no project). On the other hand, if the service is bought from an outside company, then cash will leave the company and it should be included in the cash plan.

Table 4.3 Example cash overview

	May	June	July	Aug.	Sept.	Oct.	Nov.	Dec.	Jan.
Travel & stay	8000		4000			4000		6000	
Purchase equipment						215000			211000
Maint								1500	1500
Consult							3000	2000	3000
Comms								12000	12000
Rentalequip							500	500	1000
Totals	8000		4000			219000	3500	22000	228750

Project costs, budgets, and cash are different presentations or views of project spending.

1   Costs structure the financial positives and negatives of a project. They eventually result in the C&B picture of the project.
2   Budgets structure the authorisation and accounting of the project.
3   Cash focuses exclusively on out-of-pocket[1] money for the project in order to control the project's effect on the company's credit position.

Cash plans take into account the exact point of time of the payment of cash (e.g. in the month that people are paid for project work). Budgets take the point in time as the fact that causes the costs (e.g. in the month that people do project work).

Good budget management prevents the project from encountering bureaucratic problems. It can cost a project manager a lot of time if his project moves outside the agreed budget limitations. He then loses the automatic OK for his project with a possible consequence that he must ask the finance director himself to sign purchases that he could previously authorise all by himself.

A good project manager takes measures to stay within the budget; by careful planning, by conservative estimations, by timely measures to reduce costs, by timely agreeing incremental budgets, and by leaving himself some leeway (a contingency percentage).

---

1   Out of pocket: Money actually leaving (or entering) the company. Contrast with intra company money transfers.

If the company is short of money (approaching its credit maximum at the bank), it can ask a project manager to reduce and/or postpone cash going out.

There are several ways to do so without jeopardising the success of the project:
1   Lease equipment instead of buy;
2   Speed up financial returns of the project;
3   Buy cheaper/use cheaper resources;
4   Cancel 'luxury' purchases;
5   Pay later.

If chances are real that a project is cancelled halfway for lack of funds, then the plan should be designed to make that possible without losing too much of the value of already delivered outputs.

4.4 Quality control

A project proposal (Section 7.3) contains criteria for 'measuring' quality which is an integral part of the output and as such must be designed and produced as an integral part of the output. This has two important consequences:
–   The person responsible for an activity is not only responsible for delivering the output but also for delivering output quality.
–   Quality control is an integral part of output control (output must fit quantitative specifications *and* quality specifications).

Interfacing between activities must also fit quality specifications. That is the responsibility of the entire team and a field of special attention for the project manager.

As quality is an integral part of the output, outputs should be reported as 'finished', only if quality specifications are also completely met.

4.5 A project team's working environment

A project team is entitled to work in a high quality environment. That is not only pleasant for the team but is also good for the project. The expression 'Quality triggers quality' means that people who work in a high quality environment want to produce high quality products. Good project managers report quality assessments of their team's working environment on time and

95

frequently. Firstly, because it shows the team that their observations or complaints are taken seriously, secondly because it brings issues to the attention of those who must initiate required improvements.

4.6 Effective project communication

In Chapter 5, we shall address the subject of reporting and presenting to the steering group and incoming and outgoing project communication. In this section we address communication within the project. Good communication is of great importance to a project team. Remember, a project is a one-off process where the steering is predominantly anticipative. Anticipation is a creative human action and works best if the humans are fed with good and relevant information.

Good communication starts with respecting every team member's observations and opinions. A team member who perceives that he is not taken seriously will not contribute his best. Contrary, a team member who perceives that he is taken seriously will continue to share his ideas and observations, and to contribute his best. In-team communication needs regular review and evaluation in the team. The objective of such a review is that members help each other to communicate more effectively.

The project manager must facilitate the effectiveness of intra-project communication. Communication is the main vehicle for agreeing on interfaces, sharing observations, assessing issues, generating, considering and discussing options, anticipating consequences, agreeing with actions and sharing information concerning results. A good project manager ensures that in his team there is a place for dialogue preceding discussion.

The project team can choose from a variety of communication facilities ranging from formal reporting and presentations to informal chats at the coffee machine. A clever project team uses the most effective communication option for the purpose. He also provides a few of the rules, standards, facilities and a clear structure for the communication in his team. Following, are several examples:

– project cupboards with an efficient and clear physical filing system and a project team member appointed as project secretary with the task of managing the filing (physical as well as electronic);

- general e-mail address books such as: all team members, steering group members, managers of interfacing projects etc.;
- standard e-mail urgency codes such as: IAR = immediate action required, IU = important and urgent, FYI = for your information;
- standard locations for electronic general project information such as planning files, action lists, project documentation, and project data bases;
- standard project identification on all correspondence, physical and electronic, project letter heads, reports, etc.;
- sufficient and efficient workplaces for the different types of work and communication expected in the project; e.g. some no-communication workplaces, protected from disturbance, for concentration work, places for routine work allowing for some communication, places fit for two persons closely working together, places for formal communication such as meeting rooms, and places for more relaxed informal communication;
- 'can I disturb you for a minute' rules in the project team in which the members agree when someone can be disturbed and, e.g., that one never disturbs a person at a concentration workplace;
- project information against the wall including, e.g., a print of the most recent project plan, the most recent progress report, the original terms of reference or proposal, and any other important project document;
- communication procedures for outgoing and incoming information in order to ascertain that everyone is kept fully-informed.

5 Progress Reporting and Line Communication

Learning objectives

Chapter 5 clarifies the role of communication and reporting to steering group and company management. Good communication and reporting keeps the decision-makers well informed and helps to keep the project in politically and bureaucratically safe waters.

After reading the chapter, the reader will understand how company management and project steering groups see a project and how they consequently act and react to events and situations concerning the project. The reader will also understand what is important for them and how, consequently, they need to be informed, consulted, and advised. He will learn how to report effectively and concisely so that his superiors always feel well-informed and are able to keep abreast of a situation without being involved in too much detail. Further, he will have learned methods to anticipate deviations from plan and to propose changes in time for keeping the project viable.

In this chapter the position of roles of project steering groups in the context of company management are explained and examples of progress reports, budget control reports, and cash overviews are given. The last section discusses risk management.

5.1 Project steering group and company management

Line communication is a task predominantly for the project manager. Good project reporting and line communication keeps the project in politically safe waters. Steering group members, directors, superiors, and line managers who feel well-informed and abreast of plans and events, will not pose difficult questions, will not raise unforeseen obstacles, and will not continuously want to interfere with decisions that the project manager can very well take himself.

Let us think for a moment from the position of a steering group member. In general, such a person has a 'big' job. Many subjects need his attention and he must use his time effectively. On the one hand he prefers to dedicate his time to the main facts of a project, so that he can effectively execute his steering task, but on the other hand, he definitely wants to be informed of important changes and of problems and conflicts. Steering group members don't like that others, e.g. fellow directors, surprise him with issues that he was unaware of. Too many surprises will make him lose trust in the project manager and cause him to go after the details himself.

The same is true for managers of departments who interface with the project or the base departments from which project team members originate (and probably will return to after the project). They start to act on their own when they don't feel abreast of the situation or when they fear that things go a way that they don't like.

Different persons will react differently, meaning that a project manager must test the waters with them; how do they feel about the project, what are their concerns, what has their interest and, consequently, what do they need to be informed of?

Project reporting and communication must simply aim at gaining the trust of higher management. It must be concise, to the point, and complete without going into details. It must also keep involved managers up-to-date about all the facts, events, and situations relating to the project that they consider to be important.

5.2 Outputs and completions

A project progress report must provide a quick and clear overview of how the project is faring. Attention will be paid first of all to the deliverables and the costs. Further attention will be paid to the plans and the possible changes. Take care to report the main facts only and to avoid details. Details are only given if they are important for the reader, e.g. if they are essential information for taking decisions that the project needs. Sometimes there are details that interest only one of them. That is an excellent occasion to contact the person personally and, while addressing the point, at the same time promote the project.

Table 5.1 Example progress report

	Feb.	March	April	May	June	July	Aug.	Sept.	Oct.	Costs plan	Costs revised	Variance
Police survey		plan actual								24000	22000	-2000
Traffic survey			plan	actual						13000	17000	4000
Admin. survey					plan	r-pln actual				42000	61000	19000
Citydesk survey						plan		r-pln		23000		
Taxation survey							plan		r-pln	8000	4000	

Reasons for variances:
A car accident rendered one team member unfit to work from April till June. The variance of 4000 for the traffic survey is for two days of an outside traffic consultant to help finish the survey. At the progress meeting of April 13, the steering committee decided to accept a delay rather than pay the fees of outside consultants. The delivery of the remainder survey outputs is delayed with three months. (See r-pln in the overview.)
The admin survey variance at 19000 is predominantly caused by an additional print run of questionnaires and booklets. These had to be ordered after the decision to interview 15% of the customers rather than the initially planned 5%. Taxation survey will be executed mainly by a student resulting in 4000 lower costs.

5.3 Budget and cash reporting

Table 5.2 Example budget report

	May	June	July	Aug.	Sept.	Oct.	Nov.	Dec.	TOTAL
Budget	20000	16000	12000	16000	16000	8000	16000	16000	120000
Actual	9000	20000	10000	34000	5000				
Budget to date	20000	36000	48000	64000	80000	88000	104000	120000	120000
Actual to date	9000	29000	39000	73000	78000				78000
Est-to go						9000	22000	21000	52000
Plan						87000	109000	130000	130000
Variance	11000	7000	9000	-9000	2000	1000	-5000	-10000	-10000

Budget and cash reporting informs the steering group and higher management about the financial situation of a project. Again it is important to stick to the main facts and not report details unless they serve a deliberate purpose.

Budget reports are often inputs for company financial statements, which specify exact format and coding.

5.4 Risk management

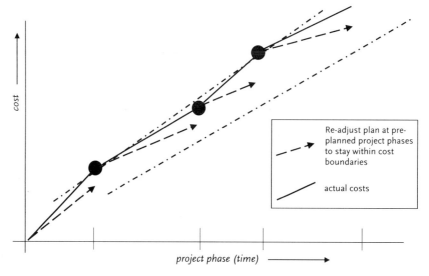

Figure 5.1 Risk management

Figure 5.1 shows how a project can be kept within cost limits by re-assessing the situation at preplanned points.

The plan must cater for decisions to control the costs, e.g., by defining independent parts that can be added or cancelled without consequences for the rest of the project.

Often, it is difficult to get a good estimation of what a project will cost and what the exact benefits will be, e.g., if parts of the project are still unsure. In such a case, it is wise to design flexibility into the plan. That flexibility comes for instance from taking an output-driven, first priority work breakdown. This is the easiest way to ensure that output parts can be added, cancelled, enhanced, or simplified.

Example

Example from the citizens' satisfaction survey (Section 3.1): Plan the target surveys as independent sub-projects and prioritise them in order of importance.

Priority Survey

1 all police services
2 counter services, civil
3 redeployment education for mobility handicapped persons
4 counter services, unemployment aid
5 counter services, housing and construction
6 redeployment education for unemployed industry workers
7 counter services, city planning
8 counter services, taxes
9 education, schools
10 education, library
11 counter services, administration

If the project overruns its budget, then the least important ones can be cancelled.

Other ways to manage risk is to approach the project in an iterative way, e.g. first produce a small pilot project, use what has been learnt to produce a larger one and, only if all uncertainties are solved, go on to produce the final full-size project. Another way is to provide output for the different stakeholders.

An example of the last possibility: A bank wants to implement a new counter transaction system. By implementing the system region by region, they can slow down or speed up the process depending on the available capacity and/or funding.

All this is sound common sense as well as sound behaviour concerning decision-makers. The steering group of a project that runs late and over budget will not be pleased if the only choice left is to go on and accept the overspending or to cancel the whole project.

5.5 Standard (written) reports

Reports that are repeated every month, at every meeting, or are otherwise produced on a regular basis should have a fixed lay out. With a standard report, the recipients know beforehand what they can expect and know that they can find the items they are interested in quickly. This way, the communication purpose for the project and for the recipient is served in a most efficient way, and results in a win-win for project and recipients.

Candidates for standard reports are: progress report, budget and cash report, minutes of project team meetings, minutes of steering group meetings, and a monthly update for the personnel information board. Regular standard reports belong to the expected output of a project team.

There is also a downside; a standard report must necessarily serve many persons at the same time. People have different backgrounds and areas of interests and, consequently, will want to see different items and different levels of detail. Necessarily, standard reports contain an average amount of detail of the average items of interest. The consequence for the individual reader, is that a standard report contains too little information of the subjects he is interested in and too much information about what he is not interested in.

The solution for this dilemma is to combine the standard reporting with other ways of communication for the individual persons and the special items. Think of a verbal account, an extra e-mail, an additional details report 'on demand', etc.

5.6 Escalation procedures

Escalation is the process of involving the higher authorities in the company when a project runs into problems for which the solutions needed are outside the capacity or the mandate of the project team.

Escalation procedures can be triggered by the judgement of the project manager as well as by agreed predefined situations for which criteria have been fixed.

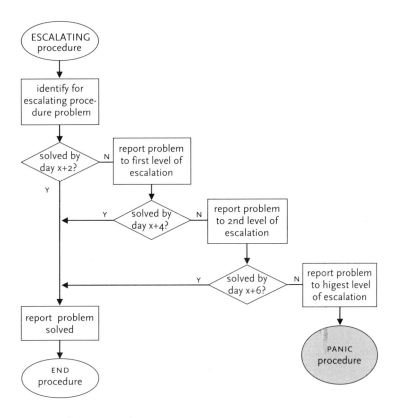

Figure 5.1 Escalation procedure

Example

A project to measure the contamination of groundwater in an industrial area on the order of a department of a local authority that is responsible for granting a yearly, renewable licence.

The project team must have free access to all areas and premises in order to take samples and to carry out soundings.

An escalation procedure would be valid in case a company denies access to the team or otherwise obstructs the sampling and sounding. The levels of escalation could consist of (1) the manager of the department, (2) the director of the local authority, (3) the major of the city.

When things are really going wrong, the PANIC procedure could be evoked to stop the company's operation, e.g. to withdraw a city licence.

6 Reasons for Success and Failure

Learning objectives

This chapter gives an insight into the reasons why projects fail or succeed and suggests sound approaches to using the insight for increasing the chances for success. After reading it, the reader will be aware of the dangers for a successful completion of a project. He will have learned to understand the project manager's responsibility to assess early if a project is viable and if reasons for failure are present. He will understand that in a company, every project is perceived as a change and will better understand the reasons for resistance to change. The effective approach to change entails the consequent involvement of those who will be affected by the change. A model of the three realities – objective, bureaucratic, and political – is explained in more detail and their observable and not so observable aspects are elucidated.

Also contained in this chapter is a list of the most frequently occurring reasons for the failure of projects. Suggestions for effectively coping with resistance are explained together with an approach to ensure that a project takes into account the bureaucratic and political situation of a project within the contexts of company and stakeholders.

6.1 The most important reasons for the failure of a project

The reasons for failure in descending order of importance

Source   authors' observations

Environment   administrative and information projects, information and knowledge of workers

1   No mission (just plan and start), wrong mission (political, subjective), or impossible mission.

2   Lack of CLOS and CLOSE (team members are kept unaware of project objectives, outputs, and situations).

3   Early cancellation (management get cold feet).
4   Complexity ignored (insufficient measures taken to reduce complexity).
5   Resistance to the project being executed ignored (resistance to the project team members who tell how it will be in the future) or to the changes caused by the implementation of project outputs (fear of change, resistance to change).
6   Lack of a mandate and resources (management makes too many decisions and does not provide enough resources).
7   ...
8   ...
9   ...
X   Bad performances by the team members

The project manager must take the appropriate corrective actions when reasons for failure are encountered.

The person who is assigned as the manager of a project with a wrong mission or for which the mandate and resources are not sufficient, is in a difficult position. The choice is more or less limited to a refusal or later taking the blame for a failed project. It is better to refuse! Firstly, because wise management will not ignore the message behind an experienced project manager refusing to lead a project, secondly, because the eventual damage he incurs for a refusal is far less than the damage for a failed project.

> Evaluation reports of failed projects exist where all the blame was placed on 'insufficient commitment of future users'. This can be seen as, a poor excuse for inadequate project management. To gain commitment from future users is a very important task that most certainly must be part of the project! If there is no way of obtaining commitment, then the change is probably wrong. If it must be pushed through by force, be prepared for many possibilities of failure.

6.2 Change management

A project is a change in a company:
- The project team members change from the work they did before to work on the project.
- The future users of the outputs of the project appreciate a change because the project team is doing something that will affect their jobs.

- The people around the project team's working location appreciate a change because the team has entered their domain.
- Some people in the company will fear that their jobs will be affected, even if that is not really the case.
- The project changes the competition for company resources.

Even today in The Netherlands, with the *polder-model*[1], openness and its associated involvement at a peak, incredibly resistance to change is often still neglected or attacked with force rather than with sensible, timely, and reliable communication and involvement. Big changes are catapulted out, surprising everyone in and outside the company. Associates feel left out or abandoned. 'It will happen anyway. How we feel is of no consequence. There is no time left for other solutions even if they are better.' People feel that their only choice is to swallow hard or to leave. It is no wonder that resistance builds up.

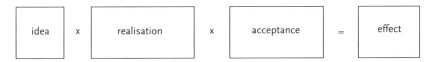

Gain high acceptance
by giving the task of creating the idea,
developing and designing the realisation,
and the continuous improvement of these,
to the people who must effectuate the change.

Figure 6.1 Effective change

Change triggers resistance

Indeed, change triggers resistance, but people will not resist a change if they know what is going to happen and if they like it. The message is clear: A change must be good, well explained, well sold, and well executed. And in a real *polder-model* change approach, the design and realisation of the change is shared as much as possible with those who will feel the effects of it (Figure 6.1).

Large companies are more difficult to change than small companies. In a small company, one person can make a big impact – certainly if this person has a lot of power and most certainly – if he is the owner. In a big company, bureaucracy, politics, and networking play a more important role and can become so powerful that even the owner (if there still is one such person) finds it difficult to effect change.

The challenge is to find effective ways to change inert, large companies.

It is easy to push a small boat in another direction.

It is strongly advised to push the controls rather
than the stern of a supertanker.

Figure 6.2 Different change approaches required

6.3 Politics and bureaucracy

The three-realities-model suggests that the success of a change depends upon three realities.

1   The *objective* reality.
2   The *bureaucratic* reality.
3   The *political* reality.

Three realities

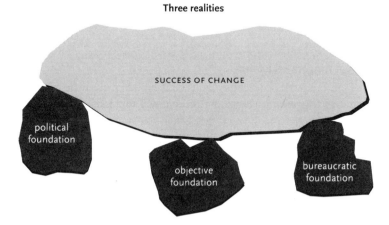

Figure 6.3 Foundation under the success of a change in big companies

It is a mistake to assume that bureaucratic or political resistance will just go away because of objective arguments.

Observable, and not so observable aspects of realities:
–   The aspects of objective reality are, on the one hand, the relevant facts, figures, assumptions, and models and reasoning that have been used and, on the other hand, the feelings and opinions of the knowledgeable people (involved, committed or expert). The aspects of objective reality are, in general, rather clearly observable.
–   The aspects of bureaucratic reality are the procedures and guidelines that rule the company and for which custodians have been appointed to ensure proper adherence. Think of decision-making, financial (cash, budgets, placing orders, signing contracts), external relations, legal, ICT etc. The aspects of bureaucratic reality are clearly observable.
–   The aspects of political reality include divisional and personal agendas of those who have power. They are not clearly observable. They must be discovered by means of intimate communication, informal contacts, lobbying, personal relation-building, and networking.

Unfortunately, it is not sufficient just to have an objectively good and sound case to get general support for a project in a company. The more impact the project will have, the more other elements and players will come into play. If not properly handled, the other elements can lead to the failure of the project.

A project, or any other plan for a change, that is based upon careful weighing and reasoning of reliable information and trusted opinions, can be enough for taking decisions in a small company but not so in larger ones. Indeed, although all the relevant material is available and is considered, the bureaucracy will not take it into consideration if the proper procedure is not followed and if not all information is produced in the proper format.

Even when the objective reality and the bureaucratic reality are covered, politics can still stop the show. If the powers-in-play have not been properly involved in the change, or if they feel that their agendas are better served otherwise, then they will not allow the change to start. This even works to the point that the powers behind a political reality can forge and overrule the bureaucratic reality and start a change, even though there is no objective reality. In that case, the change will start but will probably never produce a positive result.

The success of the start of a change depends upon the political reality and the success of the result depends upon the objective reality, while the ease of operation of the change project depends upon the bureaucratic reality.

Company politics can and do affect projects. The project manager must operate on three decision levels in order to make this project succeed. He must make three assessments:

1   The objective assessment.
2   The political assessment.
3   The bureaucratic assessment.

Politics are a well-established part of contemporary society and form the basis of democratically controlled authority. In democratic systems, the political situation is a clear point of consideration for any decision. Most initiatives encounter support as well as opposition and a decision can only be taken if the supporters hold the majority. If new elections turn the power situation, then a decision can even be reversed.

In a democratic political system, politics are generally conducted in the open. (*'Hidden' politics are a journalist's favourite prey.*) Politics also play a role in companies and institutes but the game is rarely open.

A company is generally an environment where power is shared. Politics is the process to gain a majority for one point of view, one strategy, or one decision. They are not necessarily a bad thing. On the contrary, good politics keep a company healthy because they enable a kind of democratic process for majority-based decision-making. But politics do sometimes become destructive. We therefore distinguish positive and negative politics. The positive or negative depends upon whether company-mutual or personal-individual interests prevail.

The stakeholder principle says that the interests of a company and its stakeholders should balance out. Efforts to put the interests of one party before the interests of others reduce a company's chances of success. Also associates who seek advantage for themselves at the costs of other associates violate the stakeholder principle.

The stakeholder principle. In order to succeed, a company must satisfy the needs of all its stakeholders in a balanced way. The principle also stands firm in the (classical) example of the company that must reduce staff in order to survive: It is in the interests of the company and all its associates that it survives, even if that means some associates must be fired. The interest of the possibly redundant associates of the company are best served when they are let go while the company still has the capability of giving them sufficient remuneration for their survival outside. Of course, the company also has an interest to safeguard the investments in its associates. Every associate let go is company capital, in the shape of knowledge, shape, ideas and skills, lost.

Positive politics. It is a proper interpretation from the stakeholder principle to state that the interests of a company and her associates should coincide. But in the short term, individual associates' interests can be conflicting while they are still in line with company interests. Those interests are best served then if the strongest and most cunning individual wins. The same is true for sections of people in a company; e.g. one section that wants the company to develop in direction X while other section favours direction Y. If X and Y are equally viable directions, then it is in the company interest that the decision for direction should not be left untaken and that one of the sections wins. It is a healthy process as long as it serves the common interest.

Negative politics is the fight for power between associates and sections in a company who want to achieve personal or section/departmental advantage at the cost of company interest.

Take care: political opposition is not restricted to the company but can come from any stakeholder, e.g. a team from the ministry of transport that does a project to research a route for a new motorway will encounter fierce opposition from stakeholders in the society group: think of environmentalists, land owners, and neighbourhood settlements.

Example

A project to design any kind of new system of allocating train drivers on the NS (Dutch Rail) would have encountered fierce opposition in 2001 when this was a conflict point between the ns board and unions resulting in nationwide rail strikes.)

Example

A project to extend a laboratory cloakroom for which a small partition of office space had to be taken up. Laboratory management had agreed with their director that the office population would easily fit into the remaining 92% of office space without violating company standards. The objective assessment was easy: evaluations of costs and benefits of the cloakroom extension, plus the costs of moving workplaces in the office. The inexperienced project manager neglected to assess the politics and saw his project turn into a nightmare. He was an easy victim to seasoned politicians who did not wish to give up their office space and most certainly not their symbols of status in the office. Though they could not fight an open battle, political arguments rarely fit open tactics, they nevertheless found ways to delay, change, question, and otherwise hinder the project. After a frustrating half-year, a very disappointed project manager, and very talented associate, left the company.

Also bureaucratic opposition can come from outside the company, e.g. a team researching a route for a new motorway needs permission from local authorities.

Example

Bureaucratic assessment is important. There is the classical example of the project that is started in the belief that the money 'will be found somewhere because the project is so profitable'. Many a manager of such a profitable project has found himself begging for permission for the smallest of purchases throughout the duration of the project.

Beware if political opponents are also guardians of the bureaucratic systems and budgets!

In the cloakroom example, the project manager should have recognised the potential obstacles and done something about them. The office associates who would lose workplace 'status' could have been consulted and probably easy solutions would have been found. A little effort at the start of the project would have prevented a lot of ineffective efforts and the loss of the capabilities and talents of the project manager.

Small companies are generally easier to overview which makes political games less possible and there is also less need for bureaucracy.

An example of a 'faked' reality

The project entailed the construction of bicycle paths through a particular part of the city while the main traversing streets for automobiles were closed. While on the paths, cyclists had priority over automobiles.

The objective was to reduce automobile traffic and to promote bicycle traffic. Because it concerned a politically attractive issue, the city council had approved the project. The plan was based upon the unproven assumption that 15 % of automobile traffic would move away from the car and onto the bicycle. The civil servant who had made the proposal was a convinced cyclist and opponent of cars and that had affected his judgement. His proposal represented what he hoped and believed. With hindsight, from the traffic measurements that were taken before the change, it could be easily calculated that, after the closure of the main traversing streets to automobiles, the average trip in-and-out of this section of the city became 15% longer. If the base assumption proved to be untrue and no automobile traffic would switch to bicycles, then the use of the car would increase by 10 to 15%. This was omitted in the report.

The bureaucratic requirements were well taken care of. Consistent with the rule that if the bureaucrats and the politicians want it, then the change will start even if there is no good objective reasoning, the project started, and equally consistent with the rule, it failed to produce good results. After the change, measurements showed no incremental use of bicycles and indeed a 15% increase in automobile traffic. A serious new problem had emerged though: that of emergency vehicles needing quite a lot more time to reach the extreme parts in the section. Almost immediately after the change, corrective action had to be taken.

The initial proposal had looked professional and convincing and the council had fallen for it but the mission was wrong. The civil servant had created a faked reality. Many years later, the situation is still not solved. The responsible political parties, some of which are still in power (thanks to the Dutch coalition system), refuse to admit a to mistake of several millions guilders. It would be political suicide. In the meantime, symptomatic fighting has cost several more millions.

6.4 Negotiating strategy

Success depends very much upon the way that partners in a project, or any other process, communicate. We have already seen that all the stakeholders count for something. They all have the choice of either supporting or being against the project.

All the members of a project team are stakeholders too. Team members, though, have a number of specific and unique extra products that they can get out of the project; think of the learning possibilities, doing work they like doing, working facilities, respect, and fun. In a way, team members can also support as well as being against the project. Why would a team member who does not feel a win-win opportunity support a project?

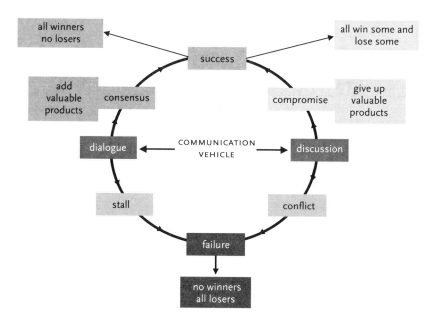

Figure 6.4 Negotiating strategy

A negotiating strategy (see Figure 6.4) based upon dialogue aims for consensus. The partners first agree the gains for the whole and within these they agree the gains for themselves. The advantage of this strategy is that a high-quality solution is more likely to be taken that will serve all partners. The disadvantage is an increased chance that the process will stall and no decisions taken.

A strategy based upon discussion aims for compromise. The partners first define what they want out of the process and then defend that against the other partners. The advantage of this strategy is that it will, most of times, deliver a solution. Indeed, the partners with the most power, or the majority, can force their preference against the will of the others. The disadvantage is the possibility of conflicts and that a poor quality solution, serving only a few partners, is taken.

7 Project Sequence Model

Learning objectives

The purpose of this chapter is to clarify the process of a project, i.e. a sequence of steps that eventually leads to producing project outputs.

After reading this, the reader should be able to structure, and put in sequence, the main steps of a project. He will understand a generally applicable process model for projects based upon six main phases: orientation, proposal, preparation, execution, implementation, and termination. He will have seen a comprehensive set of detail steps underneath each of the main phases together with advice and suggestions as to how they can be performed. He will understand the purpose, contents, and sequence of the project process, and he will be able to translate the model into specific project purposes.

The chapter contains a generalised representation of a process-driven subdivision of a project. The contents and contexts of the hierarchy of steps are explained, detailed out, and clarified with examples from real practice.

7.1 A detailed overview of the project steps

For small projects, the number and detail of phases and steps in this overview may be exaggerated while for very large projects, some steps may need to be split further and more decision points and iterations may be required. The model errs on a large project's side since it is easier to omit unnecessary steps than to start with a minimal model and invent the required extra steps.

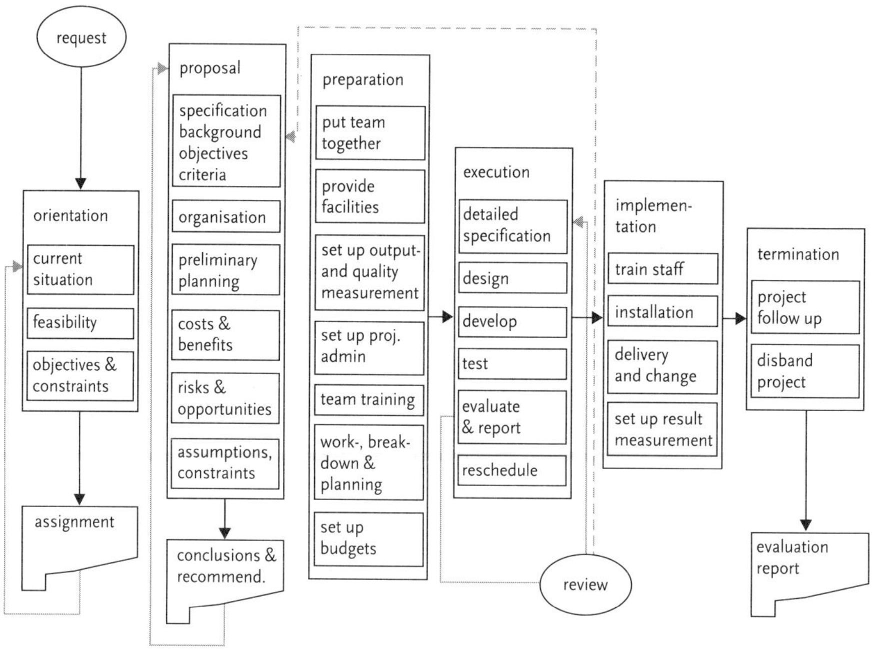

Figure 7.1 Overview of project steps

7.2 Project orientation and assignment

The orientation phase is predominantly an information-gathering exercise. In small projects, the orientation phase is often combined with the proposal phase. The output of the orientation phase is an assignment: a kind of cheap and quick pre-proposal.

Current situation

Make a quick scan of the current situation and of the changes the project must effectuate. Questions to ask in this step are:

– What are the views of the persons who initiate the project?
– What are the main outputs of the project?
– Is the pre-information correct?
– Where can additional information be found?
– Has it been tried before?

Figure 7.2 Orientation

Feasibility

Then comes a step to provisionally assess the feasibility of the project and/or to think of ways to make it (more) feasible. The feasibility step is also the place to look for alternative ways to achieve project goals.

There are three assessments to make (see also Chapter 6).

1   Objective; based upon factual information and rational opinions.
2   Political; what do the people, with the power and the interest to support or to oppose, think about the project?
3   Bureaucratic; will the project fit into the bureaucratic procedures and systems?

The question to ask for the objective assessment is: Will the project fit within the context of the company and will it bring sufficient gains in value? Sub-questions are:

1   Why should the project be done? Assess the potential outputs and their value effects.
2   What investments and costs will the project incur? Assess the potential resource requirements and their value effects.
3   What are the advantages and what are the dangers for the project? Assess risks and opportunities.
4   What changes will the project cause and who will be affected?
5   What constraints have been set for the project?
6   What preliminary conclusions can be made regarding the viability of the project?

The question to ask for a political assessment is: Can the project succeed within the context of the political environment? Sub-questions are:

1 Is there opposition against the project? Who are they? Why are they opposed and what in particular are they opposed to?
2 Can the opposition be turned into support, what would be required to do so, and is that feasible and justified?
3 Will the support outweigh the opposition?

For the bureaucratic assessment, the key question is: Can the project succeed within the context of the rules, procedures, and mandatory systems of the company? Sub-questions are:

1 Will sufficient budgets be allocated to the project?
2 Will the project team have adequate authority to use the budgets?
3 Are there sufficient guarantees that team members will not be pulled out of the project?
4 Will mandatory systems or procedures be alleviated that would otherwise hinder the project too much?
5 Will the project timely receive any legal and/or otherwise mandatory required licences, agreements and permissions?

Take care, bureaucratic opposition can also come from outside the company.

Objectives and constraints

Objectives and constraints refer to the company fit of the project (see Section 1.7). Will the project fit within the common restrictions the company sets itself? Will it fit the style and culture, the norms and standards, the rules and procedures, and will it fit into the company's general infrastructures and systems?

The objectives and constraints step also serves to describe the objectives, restrictions and limitations that are set out for the proposal. What are the rules for the team? Who can they contact and who not?

The assignment document

The final step of the orientation phase is to produce the assignment, the reference paper for making the proposal. It contains the findings of the preceding steps plus a global action plan and an estimate of how much the proposal phase will cost, when it will be ready, and what help is required from other departments, etc. The assignment report is a contract for the proposal phase.

7.3 Project proposal

The assignment and proposal phases are often integrated. There is a reason, though, to look at assignment and proposal as two different phases. In the assignment phase, the objective is to assess the context of a project and to create the conditions in which a project can succeed. In the proposal phase, the assignment objective is enhanced with clearly defined contents, organisation, and justification for the project.

There is a large list of words and expressions in use for the same proposal phase including: agreement, contract, tender, quote, terms of reference, bid, offer, proposition etc. There are also a variety of interpretations and meanings. We will leave the differences for what they are and concentrate upon the contents and process of the proposal.

The proposal phase must result in material on the basis of which a decision can be taken to go on with the project. The last part of this section contains an outline for a proposal document.

Figure 7.3 Project proposal

Specification

The specification step starts with a detailed investigation of the starting point for the project and an orientation 'on location'. It entails a description of the background of the project, which also includes a summary of the findings from the assignment phase such as alternatives considered but rejected and the results of previous attempts and the reason why they failed.

The objectives of the project must be specified in as great a detail as possible and must cover the descriptions of the primary results (products) that the project will produce as well as the valuable secondary ones. Also, the preliminary descriptions of the way that outputs will be measured are defined here; the criteria for measuring output quantity and quality.

Organisation

The organisational step of the proposal phase entails details of to how the project team will be set up:

1   The composition of the project team in generic terms, e.g., the numbers, and the required knowledge, skills, and capabilities. Probably the proposal will also already suggest persons by name, e.g. a project manager or a specialist in a key area for the project.
2   The working location for the project team and the facilities they will have.
3   The information and communication procedures that will be operational between the project team and regular departments in the company and/or other projects.
4   How the project will link into standard company infrastructures and procedures such as budgets, ICT networks, and appraisal procedures for team members.
5   It describes the project decision-making and reporting procedures with the main decision-making points. Often, the decision-making rights are worded in exclusive terms; decisions that the project team *cannot* take and for which they must involve the steering group or another authority.

Preliminary planning

The planning step of the proposal provides for a preliminary subdivision of the project into segments and the planning of these while already roughly indicating which of them can run in parallel, which milestones can be defined, and what the critical path will be. Each of the preliminary segments must be described briefly. The preliminary plan must also show the segments' requirements and prerequisites, such as resources, people, systems, machines, facilities, and required outputs from other segments. The preliminary planning must be presented in an easy to understand way, e.g. a Gantt chart (see Chapter 3).

Costs and Benefits

Costs and Benefits (C&B) form the value-assessment or justification of the project. Costs encompass all the value losses caused by resource consumption of the project.

Note that sometimes the use of resources results in a positive value result, e.g. by applying knowledge the company will probably gain more knowledge and by allocating people to projects, they will consume labour (time) but gain skills, knowledge, and shape.

Benefits are the value gains of the project. They derive from a product exchange that results from the project. What are the output products? Which stakeholder will benefit? What rewards will the company receive and what are the consequent value results for company resources?

In the proposal phase, often it is not yet possible to work out costs and benefits in great detail and accurately. Also often it is not possible to express all costs and benefits in money or other quantifiable terms. It is therefore advised to describe the elements so that the weighing-up by the decision-makers is facilitated. (See Appendix 1 'measure value') Company rules will probably require that the project also be assessed against standard company investment criteria, e.g. payback period[1], internal rate of return (IRR)[2], return on total assets (ROTA),[3] and return on investments (ROI).

Often, it is wise to show the 'best and worst case' C&B overviews with assessments of risks and opportunities surrounding the project.

---

1   Payback period; Period of time required for project profits to pay for project costs.

2   IRR; Internal Rate of Return; financial profits of the project are considered as interests paid for the capital invested in a project. The IRR is the calculated average yearly interest rate. Many spreadsheets have IRR and ROI functions.

3   ROTA: Return on Total Assets; financial profits divided by total asset value. The effect of a project is shown as the effect on ROTA, ROTA with and without the project. ROI: Return On Investments: project profits over project investments.

Example

Cost and benefits of a project to open a new bus line (all amounts in shown in Tables 7.1 and 7.2 are '000 Euros). The main project investments consist of the purchase of rolling equipment (23 buses) and road preparation (118 bus stops and a terminus station). The one-off benefit is a free-of-interest loan by the national authorities, which must be paid back in the following four years.

Intangible benefits:
1   The new bus line opens future options to connect with a sister company in the South of the country.
2   The new terminus will serve as well for future planned bus lines.
3   National coverage and market share increases with 0.5 to 8.5%, hence improving the attractiveness of advertising.

Table 7.1 Example of a six-year project overview

Most likely scenario	Project	Year 1	Year 2	Year 3	Year 4	Year 5	Year 6
Project costs	-4900						
Running costs	-200	-800	-900	-1000	-1100	-1200	-1200
One off cost/benefits		1200	-300	-300	-300	-300	
Running benefits		1100	2700	3500	4000	4000	4000
Total	-5100	1500	1500	2200	2600	2500	2800
Cumulative	-5100	-3600	-2100	100	2700	5200	8000

The most likely payback period for the project is three years. The IRR is 31%.

Risks and opportunities

Risks and opportunities describe the potential dangers and options for the project. Dangers that cannot be avoided but will not necessarily happen, can be shown as worst-case scenarios. Opportunities that may present themselves, although not certain, are presented in best-case scenarios.

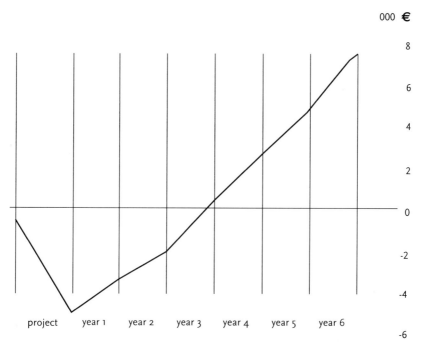

000 €

Figure 7.4 Graphical registration of a six-year project outlook

In the new bus line example:
One worst case is, amongst others, based upon the scenario where permission to install bus stops in the shopping centre is not granted and the bus lines must circumvent the centre.

Table 7.2 Worst-case payback period for the project is six years. The IRR is 3%

Worst case scenario	Project	Year 1	Year 2	Year 3	Year 4	Year 5	Year 6
Project costs	-6000						
Running costs	-200	-1000	-1100	-1200	-1300	-1400	-1400
One off costs/benefits		1200	-300	-300	-300	-300	
Running benefits		800	2000	2500	3000	3000	3000
Total	-6200	1000	600	1000	1400	1300	1600
Cumulative		-5200	-4600	-3600	-2200	-900	700

The proposal must also describe the risks (and potential opportunities) of project-induced change that can be expected and indicate how the team expects to cope with it. Project-induced change is all the changes that stakeholders will feel as the result of a project. Project-induced change can be subdivided into two parts:

1. Change felt from the fact that the project and/or the project team exist. If a project team resides in the same premises as a department, then that department feels a change, probably combined with some disturbance.
2. Change felt from the output of the project. The people in a department for which a project must design and develop a new procedure, will know that a change will come and may already fear it before any information about the change is provided.

Sometimes changes are already assumed by people when they hear the title of a project. Think of the 'office relocation project', 'effectiveness survey in the sales department', or 'reorganising the management structure'. A wise project manager makes sure that potentially affected people receive sufficient and correct information before they hear the rumours.

Project boundaries

Assumptions, conditions, and constraints set the boundaries for a project and serve for agreeing the mandate for a project team. They are negotiated and specified in the proposal phase because they affect the following phases of the project. Conditions and constraints are the limitations within which the project must manoeuvre. Assumptions define the state of decisions or conditions that are not yet definite but the project cannot wait any longer. They should no longer exist at this phase, but they are sometimes unavoidable. Any remaining assumptions are therefore a risk to the project, which will start to consume resources while an assumption can prove to be untrue at a later point in time.

Unavoidable assumptions must be stated together with the consequences in case they do not come true.

Common company constraints do not need to be specified separately for a project although they are things to be taken into account, e.g. as with a company rule that only internal financing is allowed (no bank loans).

Example

Example: constraints for the launch of a new brand of beer. The new product shall never be offered or sold at a lower price than the standard minus 3%. And: The new product shall only be transported at a temperature of 4° C in cooled trucks.

Example assumptions: for the launch of a new brand of beer, we assume that the legally required certification for the new product is granted before June next year. If the certification is not granted in time, then the launch of the new branded beer cannot continue and some of the costs already incurred may be lost.

An assumption for a project to produce course material for a university. We assume that before April, it will be decided that all material must be in the English language. If on that date, it is decided that the material must be in Dutch, then the efforts already made are wasted.

Conclusions and recommendations

The last step of the proposal phase is to state the conclusions and recommendations. It describes the reasons why the selected alternative was chosen to achieve project goals plus the reasons why alternative ways were rejected.

It is important to describe the consequences of doing nothing. This obvious alternative is often forgotten but nevertheless very important. Indeed, the decision to go on with a project is not a choice of investing or not, but a choice between the consequences of carrying out the project, the consequences of doing alternatives, and the consequences of doing nothing.

Recommendation must contain a statement to ensure a proper follow-up of the project. For example, when the project must produce a means for another project. The follow-up project and the consequent actions to be taken in the execution and delivery phases must be described in global terms. This step is important. If the project does not plan a follow-up of the project, then there may be no follow-up at all. There are many examples of research projects that were never followed up.

Conclusions must be as factual as possible and avoid opinions of the project team as far as possible. The best form is to state each time the combined observations and the conclusions derived from them.

Table 7.3 Example conclusions

Observation	Conclusion
Permission for the subsidy of 1.2 million is granted. Permission to route the new bus line through the new centre will be granted according to the spokesmen of the two majority parties on the city council. The new bus line therefore will not have to circumvent the center and may carry passengers to and from the shopping centre and the railway station.	Costs and benefits can be taken from the most likely scenario and show a payback period of 3 years and 33% IRR. To the standards of our company, the project is therefore financially feasible

If that is a sensible thing to do, it is advised to include shared conclusions and recommendations in the proposal. The wise project manager tests the water before he presents a proposal in order to judge (and if needed to influence) the support or opposition for a recommendation. One reason for not making a single recommendation can be that the political situation is unclear or ambiguous. Then the project manager should avoid compromising his rapport with the decision-makers who may have different preferences.

Still, the project manager must make sure that a good decision can be taken efficiently which he can promote by presenting descriptions of all possible scenarios and their value consequences (e.g. with the help of value-assessment forms, as in Appendix 1).

Presenting the proposal

If the project is important, the future project manager will most likely be invited to present his proposal formally. Depending upon the importance of the project, the audience may vary from departmental management to the board of directors. It is a great opportunity to gain support for the project as well as an opportunity to make a good impression on one's peers. But it can go wrong.

Think for a moment of an important member of the presentation audience as a person with power and as a decision-maker. In a large organisation, such a person typically sits in this probably regular meeting for half a day every one or two weeks. The meeting will probably have a large number of items on the agenda; company finances, people issues, brand and product reviews. There may also be a strategy discussion and one or two project presentations. Many items require decisions and many decisions involve spending company resources. The experienced decision-maker has learned long ago that however much information is presented, it can never paint the whole picture. He will try to understand the information but he will also observe the person presenting the item. Practise shows that he will base his decision for a considerable part upon how he feels about the person. Can the presenter be trusted to make good use of the company resources?

Let us return to the position of the project manager. The above observation makes it clear that he must use the presentation primarily to earn the trust of his audience. How that is achieved differs from item to item and person to person, but there are a number of things that generally instil trust. The presenter must demonstrate commitment, drive, competence, and flexibility. He must also demonstrate that he is keeping abreast with the subject and knows the facts and figures. And, of course, he must use the time allotted to the presentation effectively and make effective use of presentation aids.

The three-step presentation structure has proven its value many times. A capable presenter uses it to reach a consensus before having to revert to compromise. The structure fits the listeners' differing preferences. Those who prefer to see the facts and figures before the conclusion and recommendations, can live with the structure, since they see that there will be ample possibility to present the facts and figures in the dialogue and discussion steps. The antipodes, who want to see the conclusions and recommendations first and are interested in specific facts and figures only, like the structure because what they are most interested in is right at the front.

Table 7.4 Presentation structure (see Appendix 5)

Step 1	Tell what you are going to tell
1	overview of subjects and issues
2	what are the main elements
3	what are you going to ask from the audience
Step 2	Tell it
4	by subject; information, observation and reasoning
5	dialogue
6	what do you need from the audience
Step 3	Tell what you have told
7	review of subjects and issues
8	discussion, conclusions for the main elements
9	get the decisions from the audience

Table 7.5 Outline proposal report

Definition
    Title
    Synopses
    Company fit
    Purpose
    Primary results
    Possible secondary products
    Project induced change
    Criteria for measuring results
Organisation
    Team authority
    Team staffing (composition)
    Location and facilities
    Communication agreements
    Procedures and reporting
    Decision-making structure
Planning
    Initial work breakdown
    Initial allocation of segments to people, systems and machines
    Procedures and facilities
    Timing
    Gantt, critical path and main milestones
    Resources
    Costs, cash, budgets
Costs & benefits
    Prognoses of costs
    Prognoses of benefits
    Pay-back, IRR or similar
Risks and opportunities
    Chances/risks for success/failure
    Scope of damages and profits
    Financial and cash risks
    Alternatives rejected
    Consequences of not doing the project
Assumptions, constraints and conditions
    Project-specific conditions and project team mandate
    Project-specific constraints
    Consequences of assumptions not coming true
    Follow-up process
Conclusions and recommendations
    Summary of findings, viable alternatives, and recommendation
    Phasing of the proposal in the total project
    Recommendation for the next phase
    Next decision milestone

Outline of a proposal report

The proposal report is going to be the assignment for the remainder of the project or, in other words, the project team's next contract. The outline report presented in Table 7.5 is a checklist for a sound report structure. Of course, the outline is greatly overdone for very small projects. But even then the sequence and structure remains sound. Evident and non-relevant items can easily be left out.

In some companies, the structure and contents of a proposal are prescribed in great detail, e.g. governmental departments often insist that all their project teams use mandatory proposal forms. There are more or less standard structures in use for proposals for scientific research.

The proposal is a business plan as well as a contract and holds the somewhat opposing objectives of selling a project and restricting the responsibility of the project team.

7.4 Set-up and preparation of the project

The set-up and preparation phase of a project follows a decision to go ahead with the project, which could have been taken after the presentation of a project proposal to a board of directors.

Put the team together

In this phase, everything is prepared for the team to start with the real production work of the project. It is important to call the team members together early in the project, not only to share the work and speed up progress, but also to gain early and common agreement on the preparations. If a team is going to be crewed by old hands as well as novices, then it may be wise not to call in too many of the novices right away. Keep the balance in the team and negotiate with your experienced team members what is the best time to bring in the new people.

Provide for facilities

Proper provisions, facilities, and work places must be available for the team. If the team members must work far from home, then take care to agree beforehand their means of transportation and their lodgings.

The facilities are, for instance, desks, PCs, printers, telephones, mobiles, secretarial assistance, copiers, faxes, meeting rooms, overhead projectors, parking places, cafeteria vouchers, company credits, keys of cupboards, and access cards.

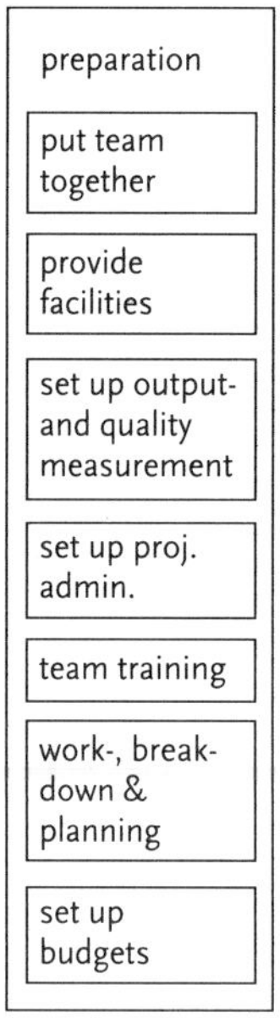

```
┌─────────────────────────┐
│  preparation            │
│  ┌───────────────────┐  │
│  │ put team          │  │
│  │ together          │  │
│  └───────────────────┘  │
│  ┌───────────────────┐  │
│  │ provide           │  │
│  │ facilities        │  │
│  └───────────────────┘  │
│  ┌───────────────────┐  │
│  │ set up output-    │  │
│  │ and quality       │  │
│  │ measurement       │  │
│  └───────────────────┘  │
│  ┌───────────────────┐  │
│  │ set up proj.      │  │
│  │ admin.            │  │
│  └───────────────────┘  │
│  ┌───────────────────┐  │
│  │ team training     │  │
│  └───────────────────┘  │
│  ┌───────────────────┐  │
│  │ work-, break-     │  │
│  │ down &            │  │
│  │ planning          │  │
│  └───────────────────┘  │
│  ┌───────────────────┐  │
│  │ set up            │  │
│  │ budgets           │  │
│  └───────────────────┘  │
└─────────────────────────┘
```

Figure 7.5 Preparation

Set up output and quality measurements

Output and quality measurements cover the criteria and measuring methods necessary for quality and outputs. The preliminary solutions from the proposal are specified in this phase. These are the criteria that will be used to measure the success of the project.

Set up project administration

Project administration entails the registration procedures and systems for the team. In this step is decided what administration must take place, how it will take place, who will take care of it, and where everything will be stored.

In large companies, there may be mandatory project and control systems (PCS) for project administration. If that is not the case, then the project team must set up its own administration. It can range from a simple manual list to using a sophisticated project management package. The team must take care to maintain a proper balance between the administration system and the size and complexity of the project. Often it is relatively easy to make a customised spreadsheet with the advantage that, if so required, it can easily be changed. The facts to register encompass everything that the team needs to keep track of. Examples are project correspondence, contracts and agreements, presence

Table 7.6 (T) in-team training required

		(T) in-team training required							
A project to design an ultra light composite propeller for a race boat		Team members							
Project requirements	Capacity required	Total capacity available	a	b	c	d	e	f	g
1 Associate properties, behaviour and talents creativeness, intelligence, accuracy, analysis, social behaviour, listening, energy, tenacity, communication.	PM judge-ment	Individual development programmes							
2 General knowledge and skills									
Management and leadership	2	2		1		1			
Project planning and management	2	1	1	1					
Presentation skills	2	1 (T)			1				
Facilitation skills	2	1 (T)	1						
pc usage, internet and intranet	all	all	1	1	1	1	1	1	1
Office technology, copiers, telephone	all	all	1	1	1	1	1	1	1
3 Company specific knowledge and skills									
Principles, company way of doing business, slogans	all	all-1 (T)	1	1	1		1	1	1
Organisation structures, plants and offices	all	all-3 (T)	1	1	1				
Financial control procedure, budget system	1	2	1			1			
Project control system, ,	2	2	1	1					
Purchase requisition system	all	2 (T)	1			1			
Archiving system	3	1 (T)	1						
4 Process knowledge and skills									
Designing propellers for race boats	1	1				1			
Building propellers for race boats	5	4 (T)		1	1		1	1	
5 Procedure knowledge and skills									
Moulding procedures for small propellers	1	1	1						
Test procedures for small propellers	2	1 (T)		1					
Melting and gluing procedures for composites	5	4 (T)		1	1	1			1
Etching procedures for fibres	2	2		1				1	
6 Specialist knowledge and skills									
CAD/CAM systems	3	1 (T)	1						
Statistical analysis	2	1 (T)			1				
Titanium moulding	1	3		1	1				
Working with epoxy and carbon fibres	5	5		1	1		1	1	1
Metallurgy and alloys	1	5	1		1	1	1		1
Corrosion	1	2						1	
Gluing technology	2	4		1	1	1			1

of persons, receipts of materials, purchase orders, resources and time spent on activities.

Team training

The step for team training entails investigating in detail the knowledge and skills available in the team and comparing that with the knowledge and skills required for the project. The gaps must be filled.

> **Example**
>
> A project must design and develop an ultra light propeller for a racing boat made from a composition of titanium alloy and carbon fibre-enforced epoxy. The project needs specialists and generalists in a number of fields: The Human Capacity Modules (HCM) subdivision as explained in Appendix 6 is used to define the areas for in-team training.

There are many strategies for training of which in-project 'Do-Learn-Coach' (DLC) is probably one of the most effective ones. (See the teaching and learning strategies in Appendix 6.)

Team training is also a bonus. Team members learn valuable knowledge and skills and so gain value for the company and for themselves.

Typical Human Resource Management (HRM) systems almost invariably focus upon generalised elements of individual capabilities and omit specific elements that concern processes, procedures, and specialist knowledge and skills. Therefore, they provide only part of the information that is required to assess a project's training needs.

Work breakdown and planning

In the work breakdown and planning step, the preliminary sub-division of the project in segments or parts as presented in the proposal, is worked out in further detail. (The how and what of planning is the specific subject of Chapter 3.) In the project preparation phase, the challenge is to find good points for the first-level split, subdividing the project into a couple of larger parts. Well split points are those that cause little or no extra work for interfaces, the connectors between the split parts. Good interfaces are easy to understand and slow, but they reduce the interfunction interference and make the whole project easier to understand and control (see also Section 3.6).

Example to reduce interfunction interference: A project to design an order and delivery system of 10 functions. A function is, e.g., to enter order lines, to check the credit level of the customer, to update order statistics, to check the availability of the products in the warehouse and to reserve them, to calculate the weight and costs, to schedule the transport to the customer, and to make an invoice, etc. These functions can affect each other, for instance if the number of products in an order line changes, then the invoice must change as well, so must the reservation in the warehouse, and the weight and costs.

Ten functions give $2^{10} - 1 = 1023$ possible interactions. If the system were split into two segments of five functions requiring between them one easy-to-understand and slow interface, then there would only be $2 \times (2^5 - 1) + 22 - 1 = 65$ possible function interactions. The number of possible interactions is reduced by 93%, hence the complexity of the project is very much reduced.

In the order and delivery example, the easy split point could be at 16.00 hours every day. Until 16.00 hours, orders are entered. After 16.00 hours they are assembled, stock is reserved, deliveries are planned, trucks scheduled and invoices produced. The interface is simple to understand and slow; a file with all of today's orders is interfaced once per day.

Example project: Design a planning system for a pig slaughterhouse. The slaughterhouse is situated in an urban area where heavy trucks are not allowed between 07:00 and 18:00 hours. The slaughter process is therefore set up in a once-a-day batch. Pigs are collected from farms during the night and offloaded in the slaughterhouse's live storage facilities until 06:00. This allows a split of the to-be-designed planning system into three parts:
1   collect pigs planning;
2   slaughter lines planning;
3   distribution planning.

The slaughtering planning system must process the number of pigs delivered during the night and placed in live storage in the morning at 06:00 hours. This simple and easy-to-understand interface is all that is needed from the collect pigs system.

> The distribution trucks must leave at 19:00 hours. Distribution planning only needs the output of the slaughterhouse by 17:00 hours, which leaves just enough time for freight scheduling and truck loading, again an easy-to-understand and slow interface.
>
> Well-chosen split points reduce complexity and therewith reduce project efforts and they increase chances of success.

Set-up budgets

The step 'Set-up budgets' entails all the preparations that are required for the budget control systems and procedures of the company. Budget systems plan and track the spending by subject (e.g. project or part of it), by time period (e.g. by week, period or month) and by phase (e.g. planned, ordered, received, and paid).

In large companies, it is often impossible to spend even the smallest amount of money if that is not covered in a budget. The project manager must be authorised in the budget control system to spend money.

Depending on the size of the company and the type of budget control system, the project manager can have direct ordering powers or just the authorisation to create purchase requisitions. In the latter case, the purchase requisition will be transformed into an order by another (buying) department.

If the project is large, then the project manager may wish to authorise some of his team members to sign for parts of the budget of his project.

7.5 Project execution

The execution phase of the project is where all the project's outputs are created.

Detailed specifications

It starts with making detailed specifications of the outputs. In the previous section, the project was split up into a small number of large parts. The split parts and the interfacing between them were described in global terms. Now they must be specified in sufficient detail to enable the design and development of the parts. The specifications must also include detailed quality specifications. The interfaces that connect the parts must be specified in sufficient detail to enable independent design and development of those parts.

Design

Then follows a step to design original ways for producing the outputs or/and to investigate existing alternatives and to select the best ones. Also, alternative shapes and development solutions for the outputs are assessed during this step as well as alternative ways of implementing them.

Figure 7.6 Execution

Develop and test

In the develop step, the outputs are actually produced and their working, performance, and quality are tried out in the test step.

Example

In a statistical research project, the hypothesis would be specified in the design step, the construction to try out the hypothesis would be done in the develop step, while the statistical verification would be done in the test step.

Sometimes it is wise to split highly complicated projects up into horizontal levels and to start with the development of a provisional solution for the highest level (which often brings the highest value). The provisional solution, the pilot, is used to improve the usability and the value of the results. For the duration of the pilot, knowledgeable persons improvise the inputs for the pilot. When working well, follow-up projects produce final solutions to replace the pilot and the improvised inputs.

Example

A customer in-stock survey project must give guidance to a company that produces ladies' support stockings. The problem to solve is that when orders reach the company, the required delivery time is always too short for efficient scheduling of the machines that produce the stockings. The scheduler needs the information earlier. Ladies' support stockings are prescribed most of times by medical specialists and orders from special stockings shops and/or pharmacists typically contain the requirement of one or two lady customers and consist of, e.g., 96 pairs in three sizes, two models, and four colours.

The required final outcome of the project is a precise forecast of the total demand of four to six weeks ahead based upon real stock information at the outlets.

The pilot could be a simple forecast model (spreadsheet). The model would use information that can be acquired from 80 customers who have their own stock systems and to extrapolate the data to a total market situation. These inputs need to be translated from the customers' coding systems to the company's system, something that the responsible representatives for these customers can do (by hand).

Follow-up projects can develop in any direction, depending upon the experiences with the pilot.

Example

A project to coordinate the production planning of a slaughterhouse with that of a cooled warehouse for meat distribution.

The first level could be to make a top-level coordinated plan. The first iteration consisting of two planners negotiating on the basis of information derived from existing individual planning systems. The second iteration could be to make a system that optimises the combined plan on the basis of the same information. The second level could be to redesign the planning systems in the slaughterhouse and in the distribution centre in order to facilitate changes in the plans that are proposed by the coordinated plan. Also, this can consist of a number of iterations that can be taken on one at a time.

Evaluate and report

If no feasible solutions could be found during design or if the initial design assumptions as stated in the proposal document are not effectuated, the solution may be to report back to the steering group and to review and reschedule the specifications. That can also happen as result of the revision of the estimations of costs and efforts. If these increase too much, the project may not be viable any more and a review by higher authorities is required. In original design projects, it is quite normal to see several iteration cycles take place before the results are agreed upon. This review can take place after the design step and during the develop step.

If in the evaluate and report step it is decided that no solutions are possible within the constraints of the proposal, then this part of the project may be reversed or stopped, pending a review of the proposal.

Reschedule

Use the revised specifications and the findings of the design and develop/test steps to replan the project and to recalculate the costs and benefits.

7.6 Delivery and Implementation

141

Train staff

Train staff is the step that serves to ensure that the recipients of project outputs are sufficiently trained to use them. In some types of projects, this step is not important, e.g., if the outputs are self-explanatory. Think of a feasibility study for a new telephone switchboard; the output is a yes or a no plus an explanation. Very little training is needed to understand the output.

But for some projects, this step is very important. Think of a new counter transaction system for a big bank. The efforts to produce the system are almost of no consequence compared with the efforts to train thousands of counter operators.

If the output is a survey report, then probably some people must be trained to understand the output so that they can work with it. If the output is a system, then people must be trained to use and maintain it.

Installation

The installation step encompasses activities such as bringing the outputs to their final destination, setting the connecting procedures in place and all other activities that are required to prepare the outputs for implementation.

Figure 7.7 Implementation

Also included in the installation step is the provision of the proper rights and mandates for future users. Think of authorisations and initialisations of budgets.

For a survey, installation could entail the setting up of a procedure for public access to the results.

Delivery and change

Delivery and change encompasses the activation of project outputs. For a new sales system, it could entail the generation of reference data, conversion of transaction data, and restarting sales procedures using the new system. For a survey, it could entail the presentation of the results. After delivery, the outputs are activated.

If the output is a new process or output that changes the ways that people work, then the change must be guided and managed. Take care, sometimes the change entails more work and requires for more creativity on the part of the project team than all the rest of the work put together.

Set up result measurements

This step entails activities to ensure that relevant measurement procedures are set in place. For every project there should be something that measures the (value-) results. For a sales system, result measurements could be added turnover, reduced costs of sales, and new customers brought in. For a survey, it could be that the result will be taken into account in a following project, at a still to-be-taken decision, or that the output is being referred to.

7.7 Project termination and evaluation

Projects are one-off processes. They have a distinct begin and end. Project termination entails the activities for a proper end.

Project follow-up
First of all, the output value must be safeguarded. If nothing is done with the outputs, then the entire project was a waste. Project follow-up activities must be planned and initialised. This is simple if the project directly produces outputs for the consumer. It is more difficult if the project is just a short step in a long chain. Direct collectable values must be collected and harvesting processes must be set in place for the indirect collectable values.

Disband the project
Secondly, the project must be formally ended. For instance, the team must be disbanded, remaining open invoices paid, budgets closed, facilities, equipment, and furniture returned, authorisations withdrawn, and access and credit cards cancelled.

143

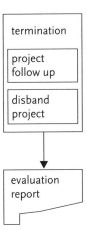

Figure 7.8 Termination

The project manager must care for his team. Each and every member of the team must have a new assignment. Nothing is more frustrating than to have no destination after a successful project. It must be agreed with them in a timely manner and not come as a surprise or when there is no time left to do something about it.

But in an unavoidable case where a person does not have a new assignment, make sure to leave project budgets open to cover his salary and report it to the steering group. Never leave someone in a situation that he must beg for a department or project to pick up his salary costs.

Team members must be thanked and rewarded properly. There are many ways: the project manager can give a party, introduce the team to the steering group and directors (invite them to the party), write appropriate appraisals, and support promotions.

Evaluation report

Thirdly, the project must be evaluated. The evaluation must cover the criteria that were agreed in the proposal plus relevant facts and judgements of factors not covered. Project evaluation is the main item of the final progress report to the steering group and is often presented formally.

Table 7.7 Project termination

Harvest results
> Collect direct collectable results
> Initiate harvesting processes for other results
> Think of secondary products, knowledge, skills, ideas, shape, options
> Document all results.

Disband the project
> People, what will they do next
> Do this timely and in dialogue
> Inputs for appraisals
> Reward and thank them
> Make a visible end e.g. a party or a formal meeting.
> Close the bureaucratic procedures and systems
> Budgets, authorisations, access and credit cards
> Return locations, equipment, facilities, desks, rooms, pcs printers, faxes telephones, portables and parking places
> Discontinue the use of services such as secretarial, travel, switchboard and mailing room
> Document all this

Evaluate the project
> Summarise criteria for the evaluation
> Evaluate against the proposal
> Summarise changes, deletions and enhancements
> Evaluate after amendments
> Review with the steering group and the recipients of the results
> Evaluate the project process
> Compile evaluation summary

Appendix 1
Value Worksheet

Assess value

Stakeholder processes deliver products for stakeholders who in return, give rewards (payment, goods, or other products) to the company. The win-win situation materialises when the two partners feel that the exchange was beneficial. But how can not-quantifiable products be assessed? Indeed, it often happens that the quantifiable exchange is very unattractive while the total exchange is felt to be very attractive. The not-quantifiable products make the difference. They obviously have a perceived value.

Let us first agree that good managers intuitively already take into account the values of not-quantifiable products when they consider the options for their company. The value worksheet will not provide a magic trick for adding quantifiable and non-quantifiable values together. The value worksheet helps to take all values into account in a systematic way.

The advantage of the structured-value approach is multiple:
1   It clarifies what the products and the rewards are.
2   It clarifies potential differences in value perception(s) and enables managers to have a dialogue and find a consensus, or to agree the differences.
3   It clarifies the condition-dependency of values in a systematic way.
4   It helps define clear statements of the values in quantifiable, 'qualifiable', and knock-out terms. It also helps to recognise hidden values through the assessment of affected resources.

The value result of a process equals the value of resources gained minus the value of resources consumed by the process. In simple essence, the working out of the equation is rather complicated.

Appendix 1.1 Value worksheet

The project to build a new, modern, and safe production line consumes money, materials, labour, facilities, and other concrete resources as well as knowledge and skills. It gains efficient production equipment. We call the value results of concrete resources quantifiable; they can be expressed in terms of money. For resources such as labour and materials that is easy but usage of facilities and equipment is already more complicated – there is not much financial difference between a building being used or not being used – but in general one will find reasonably working algorithms.

Knowledge, when consumed, will probably not lose value, it may even gain. How much is difficult to say. It depends upon many things and will be subjective; how does the owner or recipient of the value feel about it? When there is no objective way to translate the value in financial terms, we call the value qualifiable within the laid down meaning. It serves its purpose, since most people seem to understand what it means right away. The value perception can be qualified or circumscribed or put into words that describe the feelings.

The new production line will be safe; it will adhere to legal safety rules. That is an output which we call the value knock-out, there is no option, and it is mandatory. Don't think about it too much; it must be delivered anyway.

Only quantifiable values can be assessed objectively. The total value gain of a process consists of quantifiable, qualifiable, and knock-out values together and can only be assessed subjectively; to the individual judgements and feelings of people.

Nevertheless, there are strong arguments for assessing total value, albeit subjectively. Without an assessment, decisions are taken even more subjectively. With an assessment of only the quantifiable values, the decision-makers, when they feel that the outcome is wrong, may even try to manipulate the figures to change the outcome. Our solution is to list all outputs and their value properties in a structured way and to assemble the decision-makers at one meeting to discuss and assess the values. The method uses the value-assessment work-sheet.

Appendix 1.2 Value assessment worksheet

Products	Value description Affected resources, How are they affected? Quantifiable elements	Value conditions	Ko Qt Ql	Chances of conditions to occur

Receiving party

This is either the company or a stakeholder. Goods received (or required) from a stakeholder must be evaluated by the company. Goods provided to (or considered for) a stakeholder must be evaluated by that stakeholder or they must be validated from the point of view of the stakeholder.

Sending party

This is the other party. If the receiver is the company, then the sender is a stakeholder and vice-versa.

Please note that the receiver of the product solely and exclusively defines the value of a product. Value can directly result from the product and or from the way a product affects another resource of the recipient.

Appendix 1.3 Value assessment worksheet

Products	The product is the thing to receive. It can be concrete or abstract. It can consist of money, goods, information, a risk avoided or run, a capability, etc. Try to be as specific and precise as possible when entering products.
Value description Affected resources. How are they affected? Quantifiable elements	The value description describes in words the value elements of a product. Value is a perception of the receiver, therefore put here, how the receiver feels. A product can have more than one value for a stakeholder. Check against resources-list to locate affected ones. Try to quantify how much the affected resource(s) changes in value. Please put in figures all quantifiable elements and put in words the qualifiable elements. Make sure to mention the knock-out elements. Examples quantifiable: money saved, number of customers affected, days throughput time saved, stock levels lowered, etc. Examples qualifiable: run a lower risk of miscommunication, be more environmentally correct, will improve relation with authorities, etc. Examples of knock-out: best-before dates on products, financial reports to the Internal Revenue Service (tax office), Period accounts to the owners, etc.
Value conditions	Will the product always deliver a value and is that value always the same? Often a product has only value if certain conditions are met, e.g. fast delivery if ice cream is highly valued by a retailer if he sells much on a hot day in summer. It is of less value in winter.
Ko Qt Ql	The value of the product can be quantifiable (such as increased turnover or less waste), qualifiable (such as it makes me feel good because I do something for children) and knock out (such as a mandatory overview for the cbs).
Chances of conditions to occur	How real is the chance that the conditions for the value to materialise will occur? E.g. fast delivery if ice cream has a value for a retailer during a hot period. In the Netherlands, that would probably be June to September.

Appendix 1.4 Value assessment worksheet

Products	Value description Affected resources, How are they affected? Quantifiable elements	Value conditions	Ko Qt Ql	Chances of conditions to occur

Appendix 2
Output Examples from Planning Software

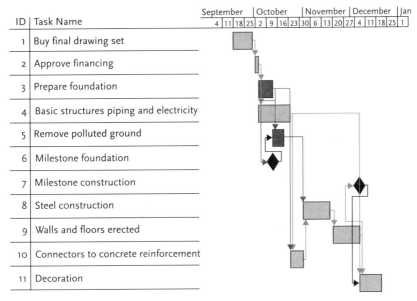

ID	Task Name
1	Buy final drawing set
2	Approve financing
3	Prepare foundation
4	Basic structures piping and electricity
5	Remove polluted ground
6	Milestone foundation
7	Milestone construction
8	Steel construction
9	Walls and floors erected
10	Connectors to concrete reinforcement
11	Decoration

Appendix 2.1 Gantt chart

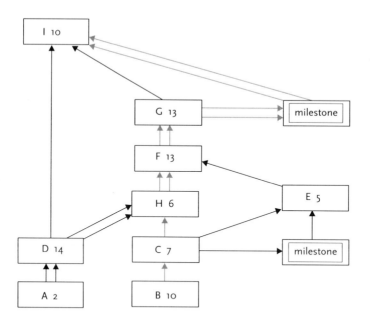

Appendix 2.2 Pert chart

The critical path is shown in double arrows.

Milestones at duration 0 days are shown as double rimmed squares or as black diamonds.

Appendix 3
Business Effectiveness Principles

The authors' education programme is aimed at improving business effectiveness with special focus on 'office' processes, with which all the various types of information and design processes are group-named as well as all knowledge and information work in general. The courses and workshops are based upon one set of improvement principles that originate from modern socio-technical views concerning the role of humans, steering based upon the generation of value, and pragmatic views concerning the role of information and communication technology.

The programme consists of mainline products for effectiveness improvement:

1   BPD for process design or redesign.
2   CI for continuous improvement.
3   PPM for project planning and management.
4   EWE for the office environment and workplaces.

Business effectiveness principles

Striving to improve business effectiveness relies upon five main principles:

1   Stakeholder value exchange.
2   Balances company effectiveness strategies.
3   Human flexibility and creativeness.
4   Continuous learning.
5   Facilitating organisation and infrastructure.

−   The first principle is to define a business role and objectives in terms of the value exchange with stakeholders. We see it as a commitment of all stakeholders to make the business a profitable and successful survivor, not only through the commitment of shareholders and management. This enables the definition of clear objectives for processes: to continuously produce the highest-valued products for stakeholders and thereby receiving the highest-valued returns (rewards) for the business.

- The second principle is to take change as an opportunity to reconsider the balances of the company's effectiveness parameters. That entails economies of scale versus clear line of sight (externally), flexibility and innovation versus efficiency and quality, size and integration versus independence, large-scale versus small-scale infrastructures, technical stability versus technical innovation, inter- versus intra-systems, interfacing and organisational rigidity versus fluidness.
- The third principle is to take humans and human-interfacing as the first step in the design of procedures, prior to the design of supporting tools and systems. It is important to understand this well because it is very different from current practice: which is to take the (functional) organisation as a given fact that defines the outlines of all human tasks. Current practice is also to use general (packages) systems that often prescribe in great detail how people must work. Current practice is the main cause for current inflexibility.
- The fourth principle is to maximise the value effects on business resources from all efforts in the company, in particular to maximise the value effects of human efforts through continuous and structured learning.
- The fifth and final principle is to support all the above with common and stable ICT infrastructures, organisational flexibility, and a facilitating management style.

Appendix 4
Warm and Cold Communication

Communication is a process for the transfer of feelings, opinions, thoughts, ideas, knowledge, and data. Communication takes place between people, in groups, and between groups. A person can also communicate with him/herself, for example by making a note of something for later use. Communication tools (technology) help increase efficiency and range. Most importantly, they enable the bridging of time and distance. Systems can communicate without interference from humans.

Formal communication is the procedural interfacing that takes place in a company. Informal communication is the unplanned, unforced, and non-procedural interfacing that takes place between humans. Sometimes, informal communication takes place because of failing or incomplete formal communication.

Warm and cold
Communication is the bloodstream of the company. Why then does communication technology sometimes bring an improvement and sometimes deterioration? Let us introduce the terms: 'cold' and 'warm'.

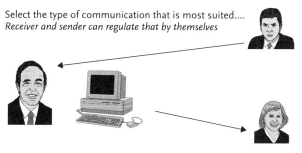

Select the type of communication that is most suited....
Receiver and sender can regulate that by themselves

Appendix 4.1 Warm and cold

- Cold communication is the transfer of concrete information.
- Warm communication is the interaction between humans.
- Cold information can easily be captured on paper or in electronic form.
- Warm information is difficult to capture.
- Captured (cold) information becomes time-independent. Electronically captured cold information becomes location-independent.

Feelings are warm, so are motivating, testing opinions, learning by copying, coaching, sharing, building ideas, reaching consensus, giving guidance etcetera. It is not easy to speed up warm communication as its speed is limited to the speed of the slowest communication, the sender, or the receiver. Facts are cold and can be transferred very efficiently in a cold way (fax, memo, e-mail, file transfer, mail, etc.). The communication vehicle used defines cold communication speed. Cold communication and warm communication are not good replacements for each other.

Warm communication is an interactive process where the entire body, and the words and actions shown serve to communicate. Awareness and control of the signals of the entire body, plus the words and actions, help improve the effectiveness of warm communication. Rather than the simple observe, feel, and act cycle, now include know, understand, judge, want, and can in the reaction cycle.

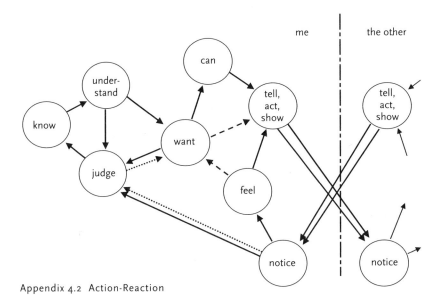

Appendix 4.2 Action-Reaction

Cold communication technology

The same terms, cold and warm, can also be used for communication technology and facilities. Communication technology has particularly opened up possibilities for cold communication. Think of voice-mail, videoconferencing, e-mail, file exchange, shared access to applications and the Internet.

Communication technology has made little contribution to warm communication. One can see the telephone as slightly warm because of the interaction and the privacy. (It loses all warmth when someone listens in.)

Sometimes it is assumed that modern communication technology enables people to be located at a distance from one another. The electronic communication facilities are expected to bridge the gap efficiently. But if the main communication requirement is warm, and it is replaced by a cold method, then the result will be a loss of effectiveness. It also occurs the other way around. Sometimes there is a desire to improve communication by bringing people and groups closer together. If the main communication requirement is facts (= cold) which from then are passed on verbally (= warm), then the result will be a loss of effectiveness.

Distance removes, to a large extent, all warmth from communication.

Warm communication facilities

Warm communication can be facilitated. In offices one could think of ways such as connected desks for shared tasks, sufficient extra space for a meeting of two at a desk, meeting rooms, informal meeting areas, large coffee corners and smoking rooms, open tables in a department. There are tools to improve the effectiveness of warm communication such as flip-overs and whiteboards in meeting rooms and large planning walls in departments.

Warm meetings, such as brainstorms and conflict meetings, become more effective with a facilitator.

Appendix 5
Presentations for Project Managers

1 Purpose

If the project is important, the project manager will probably be invited to present project proposals and progress formally to a decision-taking organ such as the board of directors, a steering group, departmental management, or project sponsors. This is a great opportunity to gain support for the project as well as an opportunity to make a good impression on one's superiors. But it can go wrong.

It is good to think for a moment, as a member of the presentation audience, as a person with power, and as a decision-maker. In a large organisation, such a person sits typically in this regular meeting for half a day every one or two weeks. The meeting will typically have several items on the agenda; company finances, people issues, brand and product reviews, there may be a strategy discussion and one or two project presentations. All items require decisions and all decisions involve spending company resources. The experienced decision-maker has learned long ago that however much information is presented, it can still never paint the total picture. He will try to understand the information but he will also observe the person presenting it. Practice shows that he will base his decision for a considerable part upon how he feels about the person. Can he be trusted to make good use of the company resources?

Let us return to the position of the project manager again. The above observation makes it clear that he must use the presentation first of all to earn the trust of his audience. How that is achieved differs from person to person but there are a number of things that generally instil trust. The project manager must demonstrate commitment, drive, competence, and flexibility. He must demonstrate that he is abreast of the subject and knows the facts and figures. And of course he must use the time allotted to the presentation effectively and make effective use of presentation aids.
The presenter must earn the trust of his audience otherwise he will achieve nothing.

2 Structure

The structure of a presentation helps the presenter and the audience to position subjects within the whole. Structure prevents questions and comments such as 'when will you talk about ....?', 'I still don't see what your point is', or 'what will it all cost?'. With a well-structured account, the audience knows what the presenter wants to achieve, what the subjects and issues are, and when they will be addressed.

An effective presentation aims for a clear goal, is designed for the audience, and has a clear structure without becoming rigid.

Structure the contents
If a project consists of more than one main subject, then the project manager must decide if he wants to present all subjects together or one after the other. If the project was to be a survey of citizen's satisfactions of municipal services, then the project manager could first present the progress of all surveys, then the costs of all surveys and finally the changes required for all survey budgets. Alternatively, he could first present progress, costs and changes of the police survey, then progress, costs and changes of the counter service survey, and then progress, costs and changes for the third, fourth, etc., surveys. There is no objective rule for what is the best in each situation. The project manager will have to use his own judgement. What will his audience understand best? What are their priorities? Some will prefer to see the subjects as a complete item (the director of counter services wants all of his area survey done together). Others will want to see their interest areas as a whole (e.g. the finance director wants to see all the costs together). If the audience contains people of many different interest areas, then the project manager can alternate focus.
That is possible with the three-step presentation structure. The three-step structure also works well for one-subject presentations.

Appendix 5.1 The three steps presentation structure

Step 1	tell what you are going to tell
Step 2	tell it
Step 3	tell what you have told

The three-step presentation structure is effective for one-way presentations. It is an even more effective way of being interactive without losing control. If the presenter feels up to it, he can have a very effective interaction with the audience. The structure helps in reducing the chances of losing control while gaining the advantage of holding the audience's attention and getting their commitment.

Appendix 5.2 Presentation structure

Step 1 *Tell what you are going to tell*
     1   overview of subjects and issues
     2   what are the main elements?
     3   what are you going to ask from the audience?

Step 2 *Tell it*
     4   by subject; information, observation and reasoning
     5   dialogue
     6   what do you need from the audience?

Step 3 *Tell what you have told*
     7   review of subjects and issues
     8   discussion, conclusions for the main elements
     9   get the decisions from the audience

Step 1 explains the process of the presentation. Step 1 should be concise, crisp and clear, and at a high level though it may be that some very important details have already been put forward. Step 1 gives an overview and makes clear what is expected from the audience. It is neither the time for detailed discussion nor for taking decisions.

Step 2 is the information giving and gathering part of the presentation. Step 2 is for informing and for dialogue. Dialogue is not the same as discussion. Dialogue is requesting and feeding information and evaluating without judgement, agreement, or disagreement. Good dialogues lead to consensus; the same conclusions shared by all.

Step 3 is the discussion, compromise and decision part of the presentation. In step 3, the presenter is the facilitator of a process that must take place with his audience. It is the step for discussion and decisions. Discussion is arguing from different viewpoints and preferences. Discussions must be solved with compromises: the opposite parties giving way a little. The better the dialogue in step 2, the fewer issues will remain for discussion. Step 3 is the time to take decisions. The presenter must do his utmost to get the required decisions taken and confirmed to ensure that the project can proceed without delay. (Recorded in the minutes, additional budgets allocated, action by others initiated, and whatever more there is.)

How to divide the time for the presentation? It depends very much on the subject and the issues, a reasonable time for each step would be about 10% of the total time for the presentation of step 1, 60% for step 2, and 30% for step 3.

3 Presentation aids

Presentation aids do not necessarily need to be the latest thing in communication and media technology. Some presenters make very strong impressions and gain the trust of their audience, by making only occasional use of a flipchart. Other presenters lost their way in spite of using high quality slides, video-ed demonstrations, and glossy paper handouts.

The presenter must draw attention to himself rather than to the overhead screen and the video station. When the overhead screen is fully lit, he stands in the dark and that is counter-effective. It is true that a picture can tell more than a thousand words but once told, the picture can be switched off and attention drawn to the real issue again: the presenter and the point he is making.

Quantitative data such as costs, budgets cash positions, profits, or stock levels must sometimes be shown with a certain degree of detail. But please remember that a figure that is not understood will draw questions and will very likely weaken the case. Understanding is easy when figures are presented top down, the top level of figures are shown first and detailed out only when needed. The method to show the details first and build them together into a whole is far more difficult to understand. Good presenters know the key figures by heart and can put them on a flipchart. But if details are specifically asked for, they are prepared to show a slide or distribute a handout. Good presenters also know who in the audience are the experts on a subject and will involve them in answering questions.

Good pictures leave little for the presenter to explain and can be understood in less than a minute. If they are really important and needed as reference for the rest of the presentation, then it is better to use an already prepared flipchart and hang it up against the wall or to put the information in a handout. Good presenters also do that with the agenda of the presentation agenda, thus avoiding questions about what to tell and when.

4   Preparing for a presentation

The audience

The preparation for a project presentation is very similar to the preparation that a good chairman does before a meeting. He will make sure that he knows who will be attending. If he judges that a subject justifies the attendance of other people he will make sure that they are invited to sit in for that subject. He will test the moods of those present to identify opposing positions and conflicting interests and to assess the support and opposition he can expect. He will avoid surprises; people don't like to be surprised in a decision-making meeting unless they are very welcome surprises. In conclusion, he will assess his chances of a good outcome and, if not good enough, he will take the appropriate measures to improve them or, in worse cases, he will cancel or postpone the meeting.

The contents

The contents must match the requirements and goals as well as the expectations of the audience. What we have discussed about structure in the previous sections also applies implicitly to contents.

The time

Estimate the time that is needed for the presentation and check that against the time available in the meeting. If the time is not sufficient? Make more time! If the time allotted to the presentation is very tight, make sure you are the first item on the meeting's agenda.

The location and facilities

Location issues can spoil a good presentation and the presenter should ask himself a number of questions and make sure that he has good answers. What is the location? Is it spacious or small for the size of the audience? Is there a flip-over and are there sufficient markers and pens? Is there an overhead projector, or a PC and a beamer if you need it and do you know how to operate them?

The presentation aids

These must be available and well organised. Nothing is more disturbing than a presenter who cannot find the proper slides. Worse even, if the beamer shows that he can't find the power point files or continuously shows the wrong pictures.

Handouts

Make sure they are concise, to the point, and well structured, as light weight as possible (two sides of the paper printed) and well indexed.

Contingency

Contingency measures will help the presenter to avoid pitfalls. What are the starting and ending times planned for the presentation and what is needed to be done to be on time? And what if the presentation suddenly is cancelled. If the consequences are bad for the project, e.g. if decisions cannot be postponed without damage or incurring costs, who in the audience must be informed about that? What if the meeting runs late and you are asked to shorten your presentation? What can be left out? Be sure to assess the time for the 'minimal essential presentation' and agree that if the meeting runs late, the choice is left open to postpone or go on with it. Try to envisage what could happen. What to do if the outcome does not go the way it was wished or anticipated?

Probably the best contingency measure is to have sponsors in the audience. Show them the draft presentation. Let them share their thoughts and views and how they feel about the others in the audience. And let them help to make a success of the presentation and to achieve the goals.

5 Do's and Don'ts

Following is a list of do's and don'ts that may be useful to remember. Although most of them are rather obvious, practice often shows that obvious do's are omitted while don'ts are not.

Don't   put yourself above the audience. Never assume that your expertise outweighs that of your audience because it will estrange you from the audience.

Don't   inform without a purpose.

Don't   go for glory or self-gratification. It might trigger opposition you don't need.

Do   use humour.

Do   be absolutely honest. Don't guess yourself out of a question because often someone in the audience knows the real answer. If you do not know, ask the audience or promise that you will give the answer soon after the meeting. Agree with the audience that the answer is relevant for the subject of the presentation.

Do   keep control of the process and the time factor. Tip: when a discussion runs too long, stop it by telling that there is insufficient time now but that you are prepared to proceed with the discussion after the meeting.

Tip: when a conflict opens up and threatens to override the subject, stop it by asking the opponents to agree how and when they will proceed the subject. Ask the meeting how it affects the subject of the meeting.

Do   involve team members. Involve them if there is good reason and make sure that it will work out well for them.

Do   dry test and try out your presentation and listen to the observations.

Appendix 6
Efficient Ways to Learn and Teach

There are many options for learning in a company. Think of in-project do-learn-coach (DLC), send people on courses, hire a trainer, self-study, etc. An overview of teaching and learning strategies is presented in the two figures below.

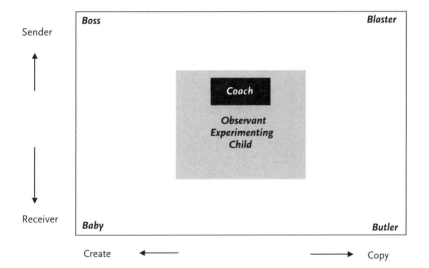

Appendix 6.1 Teaching/learning strategies

Appendix 6.2 Teaching/learning strategies

170

Language-only or text-only methods reduce learning effectiveness

A child learns generally through a mixture of experimenting, observing, and copying. Information reaches the child in numerous ways and feeling and thinking are highly interlinked. The information channels between the child and other humans, children and adults alike, are direct, interactive, and warm. It takes place through warm communication (see appendix 4). A child's way of learning is extremely fast and effective for a child. Probably it is also still effective for adults but we have stopped learning as a child.

With the ability of language, humanity has created a code for communication that has opened new possibilities. For instance, it works in the dark, it bridges distance, and it enables complicated messages. But language-only communication is not nearly as rich as the original it codifies. The ability to read and write has simplified and reduced communication even further to written-language-based communication. Additional possibilities are manifold, such as increased memory, long messages, disconnection, and distance between sender and receiver. But while language skills increased, humanity reduced or lost much of the richness and wealth of communication.

Structured, one-to-many teaching has been made possible by spoken language. Individual, independent learning has been made possible by written language. Though teaching has gained effectiveness, learning has lost effectiveness. Unfortunately, written-language-based teaching and learning is the human's current prime strategy, starting from the age of approximately seven.

It is possible to add warm ways for teaching and learning to our language-based ways and thereby increase effectiveness. The most obvious way is to teach and learn in teams where people do something closely together.

In-company teaching and learning effectiveness

In-company learning generates valuable resources for both company and associate. The first resources affected are knowledge and skills but learning does not exclude other types e.g. shape, behaviour properties and options. In this appendix we concentrate upon knowledge and skills although not forgetting the other resources. They are probably affected in a very similar way as knowledge and skills. The question is: What are valuable knowledge and skills? Knowledge and skill has value only if there is a need in the company now or in the future. The value is higher if the knowledge and skill is scarcer or more difficult to acquire.

Human resource management (HRM)

HRM aims to manage the development of the human resources in a company. In words: to increase the value borne by company associates. Current HRM focuses very much on general person properties but not enough on specific company requirements. We need a general list of specific company requirements. The next section holds a possible solution to such a list.

Human capability modules

One important preparation is to identify the recognisable elements of knowledge and skills. We call them HCMS (human capability modules) of behaviour, knowledge, and skills and relate them to both associates and to the requirements of the company. With information of available HCMS/associate and required HCMS/company, one can structure the training for the associates. Alternatively, one can look at a project and compare the HCMS required by that project with those available in the team and identify the lacking elements or the training requirement for the team.

HCMS need to be enhanced with additional data to make them really usable. Think of qualifiers such as depth of knowledge, years of experience, qualifications gained and rankings. Sometimes, some of these can be taken from other systems, e.g. personnel registration and information systems (PRIS), payroll systems, appraisal systems, personnel history systems, and potential assessment systems.

Here is a structure for HCMS that will fit associate properties as well as company requirements:

1   – Associate properties, behaviour and talents;
     – creativeness, intelligence, accuracy, analysis;
     – social behaviour, listening, communicating;
     – energy, tenacity;
     – etc.
2   – General knowledge and skills.
     – PC usage: text processor, spreadsheet, end-user database, drawing, graphics, e-mail;
     – office technology: copier, telephone communication, VC;
     – geography, demography, languages, politics;
     – international trade, global- regional- and national economics;
     – management and leadership, management techniques;
     – self regulating team (SRT) techniques;
     – ICT general: mainframes, minicomputers, networks;
     – etc.
3   – Company specific knowledge and skills;
     – principles: the company's way of doing business, slogans;
     – organisation structures, plants and offices, reporting;
     – brands and products, strategies;
     – etc.
4   – Process knowledge and skills;
     – breeding pigs, growing crops;
     – making shoes, selling cars;
     – Know about: inputs, outputs, resources, costs, markets and competitors;
     – etc.
5   – Procedure knowledge and skills (a procedure is how a process runs through
      a company);
     – procedures, measurements, use of tools and systems;
     – the general ledger system;
     – cost centres and financial accounts;
     – etc.

6   –   Specialist knowledge and skills;
    –   meteorology, genetics;
    –   bookkeeping, marketing;
    –   legislation, taxes;
    –   information and communication technology;
    –   etc.

Appendix 7
Examples for Project Work Breakdown

Project: Design a way to measure radioactive contamination in the water of the Barents Sea

Phase one: Orientation
- Assessment of public opinion and sentiments
- Research scientific publications
- Identify potential risks and dangers of radioactive contamination
- Outline a proposal project:
- Objectives
- Global action plan and timing
- Budget, resources and assistance required

Phase two: Proposal
- Specify primary and secondary outputs (results)
- Design criteria to measure results
- Design potential solutions:
    - Generate ideas for solutions and approaches
    - Assess feasibility and identify constraints and opportunities
- Select solution(s) and approach(es)
- Specify follow-up project:
    - Project organisation
    - Planning
    - Costs and benefits
    - Risks and opportunities
    - Constraints and conditions
    - Conclusion and recommendations
- Prepare decision-making regarding execution project

This is the end of the project because it needed only to design a way. Follow-up projects must cater for the execution and implementation, e.g.:

Phase three: Execution
- Detailed specifications
- Design, develop and test
- Evaluate, review and report
- Install and implement
- etc.

Project: Implement a new procedure to reimburse travel costs for associates of a university.

Phase one: Orientation
- Investigate the implementation work as described in the project that developed the procedure.
- Investigate the change that the new procedure will cause
  - Have associates been informed?
  - Is the new procedure an improvement on the current perception of the associates?
  - What benefits were identified when the new procedure was decided?
- Assess current support and resistance to the new procedure
- Propose ways to improve acceptance
- Design the implementation:
  - Specify actions
  - Global action plan and timing
  - Budgets required
- Approve implementation plan

Phase two: Implementation
- Carry out actions to improve acceptance
- Develop procedure training
- Install new procedure
- Set up procedure for problem reporting and help
- Set up help-desk service
- Coordinate the change:
    - Carry out conversion activities
    - Train associates
    - Activate help desk assistance
- Activate usage reporting
- Plan evaluation

This is the end of the project. A follow-up activity (too small to call it a project) would evaluate how well the new procedure performs and is appreciated.

Appendix 8
Worksheets

Table appendix 8.1 Stakeholder worksheet

Associates		Shareholder
Society	Company	Suppliers
Consumers		Trade

Table appendix 8.2 Barter worksheet

Company	← product		product →	Stakeholder
	Wishes	Wishes		
	Current	Current		

Table appendix 8.3 Products and resources worksheet

Product/Resource *Resource type*	Product/Resource-items
Money	
Materials	
Labour	
Finished Goods	
Half-materials	
Equipment	
Buildings	
Facilities	
Information	
Skills	
Knowledge	
Shape	
Procedures	
Image	
Brands	
Relations	
Licences	
Options	

Table appendix 8.4 Value assessment worksheet

Products	Value description Affected resources, How are they affected? Quantifiable elements	Value conditions	Ko Qt Ql	Chances of conditions to occur

Appendix 9
Glossary

Table appendix 9.1 Glossary

Above-minimum support	Value-added support, the support that delivers a value of its own. Contrasts with primary support.
Activity	A work entity, a task for a human being, a system, or a machine. Within the context of a project, it is an operation, job, or task that must be carried out in order to complete a project. An activity requires time and resources for its completion.
Agreement	A statement of consensus. *See also* proposal.
Associate	Stakeholder. A person who works for the company. The primary supplier of labour, knowledge, and skills and associate-related resources. A person who is on the company payroll or has a mid- to long term working agreement with the company.
Assumption	A statement in a proposal describing a condition that, if this is not met, the proposal is invalid.
Attribute	A data field in a data table, not being a search or a key field. A property of a key (identifier) field.
Barter	To trade with value-holding products, not necessarily restricted to money.
BEL	Business Effectiveness Loop. The cycle representing the products and value exchange between company and stakeholder.
Benefits	Gains, advantages or other values received, e.g. as a result of the delivery of project outputs.
BPD	Business Process Design. A design of a process from scratch.
BPR	Business Process Redesign. A total reshaping of a process.

Budget	Financial resources allocated to a project, department, cost-type, or other subject. Within the constraints of the budget, the budget-holder can commit resources without needing further approval.
Bureaucracy	The complex of systems and procedures to support the rules and guidelines in a company plus the people who have the task of enforcing their applications.
Business plan	A document with the essential information to support a request for financing, e.g., a project, a business start-up, a business extension, etc. *See also* proposal.
Business process	A coherent sequence of procedures or activities in a business at the end of which a sub-product or a product for a stakeholder is produced.
Cash	Money flows in or out of the company. Out-of-pocket spending. Total money flow minus the flow that stays within a company, e.g. inter-department flows.
CLOS	Clear Line Of Sight. Workers in a process understand the role of the process and their role therein.
CLOSE	Clear Line Of Sight Externally. Workers in a process understand the process outputs, the recipients of these (the stakeholders) and the rewards returned by the recipients.
Cold communication	An exchange of information, mainly consisting of status facts and/or transactions (cold information).
Communication	A process between people, groups of people, and systems to exchange feelings, opinions, ideas, knowledge and data.
Communication technology	Tools to speed up and enable communication. Also to bridge distance and time. Almost exclusively supporting cold communication.
Company	A business co-operation, with the objective of making profit. A network of interacting processes with the objective to satisfy the needs of its stakeholders. The group name representing any type of institute including commercial companies, organisations, cooperation agreements, national, regional, and community institutes.
Company fit	The extent to which actions align with the direction, rules, and restrictions the company has set itself. Concerns style, culture, standards, norms, values, rules, procedures, and infrastructures.
Company outlines	The set of company specifics. The restrictions, style, culture, standards, norms, values, rules, procedures, infrastructures, and general systems. Company context.
Constraint	Condition, limitation.

Consumer	Stakeholder. Buyer of the product at the end of the consumer chain. The consumer of the end-product. Consumer and gatekeeper.
Consumer-chain	The chain of partners who cooperate to bring a consumer product to a consumer such as: producer of raw materials → manufacturer of consumer goods → wholesaler → retailer → consumer.
Contents-driven work break down	The first priority split is into main sub-products or intermediate products. (Also called output-driven work breakdown.)
Continuous improvement	People actively seek opportunities to improve their work while they perform it. They react to changes and take advantage of freedom to improve effectiveness.
Continuous improvement cycle	SMARCT cycle, (Specify, Measure, Act, Review, Calibrate, Train).
Contract	A written and signed agreement. *See* proposal.
Corporation (Inc.)	A holding company. Often, a number of companies that share a name, brand names, a top management structure, and financial resources but sometimes sharing more (e.g. personnel and organisation and information and communications infrastructures).
Crashing	Crashing or expediting an activity in order to reduce its duration.
Critical path	The longest duration in a flow of activities when these run as much as possible in parallel. A CP leads to earliest completion time in a network of related activities.
Customer	Stakeholder. Trade partner. The next partner in the consumer chain.
Data	Recordings, most of times on electronic files.
Data base	Organised data. A coherent information set. Electronically recorded data commonly provided together with facilities for access, backup and recovery, and safeguarding of data integrity.
Data field	Information element in a data record. One column in a data table.
Data record	Group of data fields that share the same key. One line in a data table, containing all attributes of a key.
Data system	Automated system for data capturing, processing, retrieving, and safeguarding.
Demand chain	The chain of companies that forward a consumer demand. The consumer chain with reversed direction. Consumer → retailer → wholesaler → manufacturer of consumer goods → producer of raw materials.

185

DSS	Decision Support System. An information tool for decision-makers. Generally consisting of a database with history and planning data plus facilities for analysis, forecasting, and 'what if' assessment.
Effectiveness	Value returned minus costs to produce. Value generated for efforts. Value generated over invested resources. The quality of fulfilment of the needs of the recipient stakeholder.
Effectiveness of human efforts	Effectiveness = Time x Pace x Value.
Efficiency	Productivity per investment. Efforts per product. Resources invested per product
Efficiency in EQFI	Lowest price.
EQFI	Efficiency, Quality, Flexibility, Innovation. (Survival model of Bolwijn and Kumpe, 1998)
EIS	Executive Information System.
Feedback	Feed information to previous steps in the process and/or to previous occurrences of the same process.
Feedback cycle	The cycle of information about a process and interfaces in a process.
Flexibility	Capacity to change. Ease of change.
Flexibility in EQFI	Choice, variation, and speed.
Flowcharting	A process documentation technique.
Forward control	Anticipative and preventive control procedures.
Function driven work breakdown	The first priority project split into parts is per function or per skill. (Also called skill-driven work breakdown.)
Gantt chart	The presentation of a plan as activities in a time period. Activities are horizontal, time-periods vertical. Invented around 1917 by Henry L. Gantt.
Group	Team. Persons sharing an identifying property. People sharing a responsibility, e.g. for a project.
IDEF	Information DEFinition. A process documentation technique.
Improve cycle	A stakeholder process design improvement cycle. *See also* SMARCT and BEL.
Information	Organised and interpreted data. Aggregated data.

186

Information worker	A person with a role in processes that handle data (transactions) and/or generate information.
Innovation	Explore new ways. Effectuate breakthrough ideas.
Innovation in EQFI	Original, renewal, new.
Input-Process-Output (IPO)	Overview recording the interfacing into and out of a team, a process, or procedure.
Interface	A sub-product that is exchanged between consecutive teams or tasks in a process.
Interface, easy to understand	Self-explaining interface.
Interface, slow	The interfacing frequency is slow, e.g. once per day or slower.
Interfacing	Linking the parts of a process together. Linking tasks.
IPD	Information Process Design
IRR	Internal Rate of Return; financial profits of the project are considered as repayments plus interest for the capital invested in the project. The IRR is the average yearly interest rate at which the capital is fully repaid by the profits.
Key field	Data field defining the sequence in a data table. The primary key field is the most efficient search field.
Knowledge worker	Information worker. A person whose job is based upon knowledge and brainpower rather than on physical performance.
Labour costs	Cost of human efforts.
Leadership style	The way in which a chief addresses and steers his subordinates. Distinguishable styles include tell, manage, delegate, lead, facilitate, and self-regulate. See also management.
Levelling	Scheduling activities in order to minimise variation in resource usage within a certain period of time (smoothing).
Management	The (higher) hierarchy levels in a company responsible for the organisation, planning, leading and control of the operational levels.
Manager	The responsible person, generally the chief of a team of associates, e.g. a department or a project, but can also be the first person responsible for a brand, a facility, or important resource.

Milestone	A point of a main achievement in a project. Often the official confirmation that a main part of a project is completed. The interface between elements of the main work breakdown.
Minimum support	Primary support. Support to keep the primary process performing.
Minimum support game	A game to appreciate value and cost of sub-products.
MIS	Management Information System.
Mission	The purpose, the reason for the existence of a company, a process or a project.
Multi-moment time measurement	Statistical method to measure time spent by subject, type of work etc.
NAVA	Non-Adding-Value-Activity.
Negative politics	The game for power to serve individual or group interests at the cost of company/mutual interests.
Offer	See proposal
Office	A room or building used as a place of business.
Office procedure	A part of an office process. A documented office process.
Office process	A business process performed by information or knowledge workers.
Office worker	A person who works in an office.
Output-driven work breakdown	The first priority split is into main sub-products or intermediate products (contents-driven work breakdown.)
Overhead-time	Time spent on organising or facilitating primary process tasks, e.g. for setting up the tool to plan and share work among team members.
PERT	Program Evaluation and Review Technique. A planning technique aiming at earliest possible delivery. PERT was developed by the U.S. Navy in cooperation with Booz-Hamilton and the Lockheed Corporation for the Polaris missile/submarine project in 1958.
Politics	Power game. The basis for democratically controlled authority. Process to gain a majority decision.
Positive politics	The power game that serves company interests.
Primary process	Process for producing primary products for stakeholders.

Primary product	The product for the primary exchange between a company and a stakeholder. Associate: salary (for time and efforts), Supplier: payment (for goods delivered), customer/trade: packs of products (for money), Shareholder: dividends (for investments), Society: infrastructure (for taxes), Consumer: single product (for money).
Primary support	The support to keep primary processes running. The value comes exclusively from the products produced by the primary processes.
Procedure	Part of a process. A documented process.
Process	A sequence of activities to produce a product for a stakeholder. A named function for turning an agreement with a stakeholder into a delivered product and to receiving the proper reward. Also called a business process or a stakeholder process.
Process-driven work breakdown	The first priority split of the project is into the main (sequential) process parts (activity-driven work breakdown).
Productivity	Number of products per person (or per machine) per elapsed time.
Profit	Value result of a process. Value received minus value sacrificed. Value result between company and a stakeholder.
Project	A one-off process with the objective of producing a predefined result.
Proposal	A proposition for decision-makers of a project. Contains the minimal essential information necessary to commit to the preparation part of a project and to decide in principle regarding the total project. Other names: contract, tender, agreement, business plan, quote, terms of reference, offer. Second main phase of a project (orientation, proposal, preparation, execution, implementation, termination).
Quality	A rating on the scale of good and bad. The extent to which specifications are met.
Quality in EQFI	Reliability and durability.
Quote	*See* proposal
Reach	The area of influence (of a team or individual or other).
Redesign	A new design for an existing situation (business, process, work).
Reference table	A data table containing key fields of other data tables as attributes. A reference table serves to dynamically join data from two or more data tables. Also serves to speed up access to tables via attribute data fields (non-key fields).

Resources	Carriers of value. Possessions of a company. Company assets. Fuel for processes.
ROI	Return On Investments: (*see also* IRR). Project profits over project investments.
ROTA	Return On Total Assets. Financial profits divided by total asset value. The effect of a project is shown as effect on ROTA; ROTA with and without the project.
Sales volume	Total primary products sold. Can be expressed in financial terms and volumes. *See also* turnover.
Secondary process	Value-added process, Process producing secondary products.
Secondary product	A by-product with a value not being a primary product.
Segmentation focus	Split a whole (e.g. a process) according to focus properties: stakeholder, product, process, or function. Process, skill, or contents driven focus for a work breakdown structure.
Self-regulating	The power to change and improve a procedure, task, or function given to the people who execute it.
Self-sufficiency	Being able to work without the help of other people, other departments, or services.
Shareholder	Stakeholder. Owners of a company, providers of risk-taking capital. Representatives of the shareholders (board of directors of a company).
Skill-driven work breakdown	The first priority project split into parts is per function or per skill. (Also called function-driven work breakdown).
SMARCT	Specify, Measure, Act, Review, Calibrate, Train. Continuous improvement cycle. (John Thomson, GPR Consultants Ltd & Ron Asher, Mars Inc.)
Smoothing	Scheduling activities in order to minimise variation in use of resources between one time period and the next. (Same as levelling.)
Society	Stakeholder. Humanity, ecology, environment. National, regional, and local authorities and institutes, labour and employer organisations, etc.
Socio-technical	Integral application of social and technical science.
Stakeholder	Group name for the partners of a company. A partner who has a stake in the company, a trade partner. Six stakeholder groups: associate, shareholder, consumer, customer (trade), society, and suppliers.

Stakeholder principle	In order to be successful, a company must satisfy the needs of all its stakeholders in a balanced way.
Steering	Direction processes. Define mission, vision and strategies, make high-level trade-offs, lead the change and innovation process.
Sub-process	A part of a process.
Sub-product	The interim-product (interface), e.g., as is provided by one team to another. A component of a stakeholder product.
Suppliers	Stakeholder: Providers of materials, services and equipment.
Support process	Processes for supporting primary processes and value-added processes.
Survival phases (EQFI)	Efficiency, Quality, Flexibility, Innovation (Bolwijn and Kumpe, 1998).
System maintenance	Keep information systems up to date and running.
Table	Organised data consisting of columns and rows in which the contents per column are of one type and the contents of one row are a coherent set (generally identified by the contents of the column situated at the left of the row, the key field.
Task	A number of activities given to a team (or person).
Taylorian	Division of work according to the system designed by Taylor (1927). Maximal labour division. A process is split up into a large range of sequential equal time-consuming tasks. Also: take out and concentrate identical or very similar types of work and give to a specialist task group (functional organisation).
Team	Group. Persons sharing an identifying property. People sharing a responsibility, e.g. for a project.
Tender	*See* proposal
Terms of reference	A concise document signed by financier and project manager containing the minimal essential project information. *See also* proposal.
TEV	Trigger-Effort-Value cycle. Feedback cycle for VAS (Value-Added Support).
Time reporting	Register time and activities.
Time study	Detailed time measurements of activities.

191

Tool	General name for an efficiency utility. In office environments, e.g. data processing systems, e-mail, fax, copier, PC, internal mail services and presentation facilities.
Trade	Stakeholder. Customer/trade. The next partner in the consumer chain, e.g. wholesalers, commercial organisations, retailers, warehouses, superstores.
Transaction	An interaction. The registration of a fact.
Transaction chain process	Another name for Primary Process.
Trigger	The person, the instance, date-and-time, or other external event starting a process, procedure or task.
Trigger-Effort-Value (TEV)	Feedback cycle for VAS (Value-Added Support) processes.
Turnover	Total sales in a reporting period (of 12 months), equals the sum of the total invoices of primary consumer products sold in that period. Turnover is sometimes expressed in sales volumes (e.g. tonnes, m^3).
User efficiency	Efficiency for the user of tools, services and facilities. The avoidance of overheads, waste, and waiting caused by user tools.
Value-Added Support (VAS)	Secondary products process.
Value principle	Win-win or profits is derived from all types of values, not only from values that can be expressed or translated in financial terms.
Vision	A compelling picture of a future state in which the mission is achieved. Makes visible the mission of a company, a process, a project etc. A choice of how a mission will be achieved.
Warm communication	Exchange feelings, opinions or emotions. Inter-personal $\rightarrow$ synergy seeking. Communicates warm information.
Win-Win	Company and stakeholder gain value.
Workplace	The home base of an associate in his company. An office workplace (desk plus furniture and equipment).
Workplace risk analysis	Mandatory (in the European Community) survey to identify health and security risks of workers in their jobs and their working environments.
Work breakdown	Subdivision of a project in parts. Contents, process, or skill-driven work breakdown.

Working environment	The surroundings of a workplace (e.g. the office, factory). Also encompasses lighting, noise, smell, temperature, air quality, outside view, possibilities to socialise, coffee corners and cafeteria, meeting facilities, car parking, connections, etc., and the risks to health and safety they incur.
WYSIWYG	What-You-See-Is-What-You-Get. A property of PC software that allows the operator to look through the screen at a document with all lay-out, editing and printing options.

Appendix 10
Planning with Spreadsheets

Table appendix 10.1 shows a scheduler spreadsheet. This type of spreadsheet is advised when many tasks must be scheduled (put in sequence and fixed in time slots). Available capacity per week is defined plus required capacity per activity. The spreadsheet schedules the activities while taking into account additional (activity) properties such as priority, earliest start, latest completion, and maximum number of persons active. The scheduler part of the spreadsheet can be enhanced by the costs of the project. The spreadsheet can also be enhanced to show actual time spent and actual costs made.

Table appendix 10.2 shows a different type of plan. This spreadsheet is advised when the project tasks must be executed by persons with many other tasks and not the scheduling of capacity but the timing of the completion of tasks is the main planning target. The plan makes it clear when (in which weeks) a task must be carried out and completed and which persons must perform the task. A task is shown as *** *** in the corresponding week columns while a completed task is noted with an 'OK'.

Table appendix 10.1 Scheduler spreadsheet

PROJECT X — WEEKS — Year 1

PROJ	Prir	#TM	units	start	ready	ready	48	49	50	51	52	1	2	3	4	5	6	7	8	9	TOT
							#	#	#	#	#	#	#	#	#	#	#	#	#	#	*
							5	5	5	5	0	4	5	5	5	5	5	5	5	5	232
				early sched req			8	11	14	17	0	20	16	16	14	12	12	12	6	0	158
				start	ready	ready	40	55	70	85	0	80	80	80	70	60	60	60	30	0	770
Allocate manually	V	n.a.	27	n.a.		n.a.	5,0	3,0	4,0	1,0	0,0	2,0	2,0	2,0	2,0	2,0	2,0	2,0	0,0	0,0	27
Management		0,20	n.a	148		151	1	1	1	1											2
Administration		0,20	n.a.	201		208							1	1	1	1	1	1	1	1	8
		n.a																			
Chambre of commerce	7	#	1	5	20	148	5														5
Agree monthly invoicing	4	#	5	15	148	148	15														15
Initiate pay system	4	#	7	80	148	150	15	35	31												80
Set up reporting	4	#	6	40	148	150		17	24												40
Network access	4	#	5	30	148	151			12	19											3
Set up bookkeeping	4	#	4	20	148	151				20											20
Make/agree cash plan	4	#	2	20	148	202				10		8	2								20
time reg consolidation	4	#	4	10	148	151				10											10
Set up work alloc proc	4	#	1	5	148	151				5											5
Copy folders	4	#	6	10	148	151				10											10
QC procedures	2	#	6	20	148	201				10		10									20
Evaluate	1	#	6	15	148	201						15									15
prod 1-15 for 41 I 60 cntr	1	#	16	300	148	205						44	75	77	67	37					300
prod 16-30 for 41 I 60 cntr	1	#	12	130	148	207										20	57	53			130
Delivery	1	#	5	25	148	208													4	21	25
	0	#				0															
	A																				
Total allocated			752				40	55	70	85		80	80	80	70	60	60	60	22		762
spare capacity																				8	8

PROJECT X	Costs		Person-days per week														
	'000 Euro1	g	48	49	50	51	52	1	2	3	4	5	6	7	8	9	TOT
Man days grp 1		1	25	25	25	25		20	25	25	25	25	25	25	25		295
grp 2	costs	2	5	5	5	5		4	5	5	5	5	5	5	5		59
grp 3	p/wk	3	10	10	10	10		8	10	10	10	10	10	10			108
grp 4	p/man	4		15	30	45		48	40	40	30	20	20	20			308
Man costs Costs grp 1	0,53	1	13	13	13	13		11	13	13	13	13	13	13	13		156
Costs grp 2	0,90	2	5	5	5	5		4	5	5	5	5	5	5	5		53
Costs grp 3	0,44	3	4	4	4	4		4	4	4	4	4	4	4			48
Costs grp 4	0,35	4		5	11	16		17	14	14	11	7	7	7			108
Total associate costs			22	27	33	38		35	36	36	33	29	29	29	18		365

Non-associate costs

	amount	when due															
Hardware	115	205										115					115
Software	98	206											98				98
Rentals	300	2001															
Sales old equipment	-50	207												-50			-50
Total non-associate costs												115	98	-50			163
Totals project			22	27	33	38		35	36	36	33	144	127	-21	18		528

Table appendix 10.2 Delivery control spreadsheet

Team members	pp Peter P	
	nb Niels	
PROJECT	tj Tonnie	Passed weeks shaded
Monitor SRT CS	nr Natascha	
	pd Peter D	
	aw Ad vdW	Periods of four weeks →

		Responsible person	pp nb tj nr pd aw	L I	prev done	1 2	1 3	1 4	1 5
		Activity	Date Monday week 1	N K		29 1 1	26 2 1	26 3 1	23 4 1 1
1	1	Planning project		#					
1	2	-		#					
1	3	Terms of Reference	aw	#	ok				
1	4	Set up report structure PP	pp	#	ok				
1	5	Set up report structure NB	nb	#		******OK			
1	6			#					
1	7	Planning PP + NB	pp nb	#		- - - - - - -	******		
1	8	Zero measument		#					
2	9	-		#					
2	10	Concept zero report	pp nb	#		- - - - - - -	OK ***		
2	11	Input Periodreport P12 98	pp	#		- - - - - - -	******		
2	12	Interview TJ, NR, etc.	pp	#		- - - - - - - - -	******		
2	13	Add additional services by CS	pp	#		- - - - - - - - -		******	
2	14	Zero-measurement report	pp	#		- - - - - - - - -		***	
2	15	Agree with steering group	pp tj pd aw	#		- - - - - - - - - - -			***
2	16			#					
2	17	Self-regulating team activities		#					
3	2	-		#					
3	3	Inventory by end of year	pp	#		- - - - - -	***	OK	
3	4	Set up documentary system	pp	*		OK			
3	5			#					
3	6	Per SRT initiative		#					
3	7	Set up document system	pp	#		- - - - - - -	****** ****** ******		
3	8	Set up files	pp	#		- - - - - - - -		****** ***	
3	9			#					
4	1	SRT theory		#					
4	2	-		#					
4	3	Learning organisation	nb aw	#		- - - - - - - - - - -			***
4	4	SRT theory/meth Avd W	nb aw	#		- - - - - - - - -			******
4	5			#					

References

Amersfoort, P. van (1992) 'Het vergroten van de bestuurbaarheid van productie-organisaties', ST-groep 92, Febo, Enschede.

Baker, B.N. and Eris, R.L.(1964) *An introduction to PERT CPM*, Irwin, Homewood, IL.

Bertrand, J.W.M., Wortmann, J.C. and Wijngaard, J. (1990) *Production control - A structural and design oriented approach*, Elsevier Science Publishers, Amsterdam.

Bolwijn P., and Kumpe, T. (1998) *Marktgericht ondernemen: management van continuïteit en vernieuwing*, Van Gorcum, Assen.

Buchanam, D. and Boddy D. (1992) *The experstise of the change agent: public performance and backstage activity*, Prentice-Hall, Englewood Cliffs.

Buttrick, R. (1997) *The project workout*, Financial Times Management, London.

Campbell, A., Divine, M. and Young, D. (1990) *A sense of mission*, Financial Times/Pitman, London.

Campbell A. and Tawadey, K. (1993) *Mission and business philosophy*, Butterworth-Heinemann, London.

Dean, B.V. (1985), *Project management, methods and studies*, Elsevier, New York.

Eijbergen, R. (1999) *De invoering en het effect van zelfsturende teams in organisaties*, Lemma Utrecht.

Eijnatten, F.M. van (ed.) (1996) *Sociotechnisch ontwerpen*, Lemma, Utrecht.

Emery, F.T. and Trist, E.L. (1965) The casual texture of organizational environments. *Human Relations*, 18 (1).

Freeman, R.E. (1984) *Strategic management: a stakeholder approach*, Pitman, London.

Galbraith, J.R. (1973) *Designing complex organizations*, Addison-Wesley, Englewood Cliffs.

Sibbit, D. and Drexler, A. (1992) *Graphic guide to best team practices*, Graphic Guide Inc., San Francisco.

Hammer, M and Champy J. (1993), *Reengineering the cooperation*, Harper-Collins Publishers, New York.

Hamel, G. and Pralahad, C. (1989) Strategic intent, *Harvard Business Review*, volume 67.

Johnson G. and Scholes, K. (1997), *Exploring corporate strategy*, 4th edn., Prentice-Hall, Englewood Cliffs.

Kaplan, R.S. (ed.) (1990) *Measures for manufacturing excellence*, Harvard Business School Press, Boston.

Kaplan, R.S. and Norton, D.P. (1992) The balanced scorecard: measures that drive performance, *Harvard Business Review*, Jan-Feb, pp. 71-79.

Keen, P.G.W. and Scott Morton, M.S. (1978) *Decision support systems – an organisational perspective*, Addison-Wesley, Amsterdam.

Keuning D. (1995) *Grondslagen van het management*, Stenfert Kroeze, The Hague.

Lientz, B.P. and Rea, K.P. (1995) *Project management for the 21st century*, Academic Press, London.

Lockeyer, K. and Gordon, J. (1995) *Project management and project network techniques*, Financial Times Management, London.

Loeffen, J.M.J. (1999) Informele afstemming in productieorganisaties; een SocioTechnische blik op informatievoorziening. TU Eindhoven proefschrift D1.

Machiavelli (1961) *The Prince*, Penguin, Harmondsworth.

Meredith, J.R. and Mantel, S.J. (1995) *Project management: a managerial approach*, John Wiley, New York.

Mintzberg, H. (1979) *The structuring of organizations*, Prentice-Hall, Englewood Cliffs.

Mintzberg, H. (1983) *Power in and around organizations*, Prentice-Hall, Englewood Cliffs.

Mitroff, I.I. (1983) *Stakeholders of the organizational mind: toward a new view of organizational policy making*, Jossey-Bass, London.

Naik, B.M. (1984) *Project management: scheduling and monitoring by PERT/CPM*, Advent books.

Nolan, V. (1981) *Open to change*, Password Publication, Westfield, Upper Ladyes Hill, Kenilworth, Warwickshire UK.

Porter, M.E. (1985) *Competitive advantage: creating and sustaining superior performance*, Collier Macmillan, London.

Sibbit, D. and Drexler, A. (1992) *Graphic guide to best team practices*, Graphic Guide Inc., San Francisco.

Sitter, L.U. de. (1982) *Op weg naar nieuwe fabrieken en kantoren*, Kluwer, Deventer.

Taylor, F.W. (1911) *Principles of Scientific Management*, Harper, New York USA.

Van Til, C., Wijnen G. and Steen, J. (1999) *Werken in een project*, Onderwijsondersteuning Wageningen universiteit, Wageningen.

Weide, A van der (2000) Stakeholder Value Analysis for Business Process Design, Course syllabus Wageningen School of Management, Wageningen.

Index

207

About the Authors

Ad van der Weide

In 2000, Ad van der Weide started his business effectiveness advisory company *OfficeScan* after retiring from Mars Inc. He specialises in effectiveness improvement for information and knowledge processes. In this area, he designed original approaches and innovative methodologies including: business process design, continuous improvement, project management and information workers' ergonomics. In his previous career, he performed managerial functions in information and communications technology, industrial engineering, logistics, and organisation development. Since 1998 he has guest-lectured at the Wageningen's University & Research Institute (WUR) and at the MBA programme of Wageningen's School of Management (WSM). In his capacity as senior advisor to The Netherlands Management Cooperation Programme (NMCP), he guest-lectures at universities and coaches projects in developing countries.

Adrie Beulens

Adrie Beulens graduated in mathematics at the Technological University of Eindhoven in 1972. Until 1980, he worked in a variety of managerial functions in information systems and operations research for the Royal Dutch Air Force and Mars Veghel bv. Until 1988, he was head of the Information Systems Department and an associate professor in information systems and quantitative methods, first at the Graduate School of Management in Delft and, from 1984, at the Erasmus University in Rotterdam. From 1988 until 1995, he was Dean of the Faculty of Informatics of the Haagse Hogeschool in The Hague. In 1995, he was appointed professor of information systems and computer science, head of the Computer Science Department, and director of Wageningen School of Management. He has been active as a management consultant in the areas of

ECR, logistics, ICT, decision support systems, E-commerce, supply chains, tactical and operational planning, and reference information models related to these.

Stephan van Dijk
Stephan van Dijk works as a management consultant on supply chain management and strategic alliances in the agribusiness and life science industry. Concurrently, he is associated with the Eindhoven Center for Innovation Studies (ECIS) at the Eindhoven University of Technology as a research fellow. His research at ECIS concerns the management of knowledge exchange processes between organisations during strategic technology alliances. Stephan formerly worked at the Information Technology Group of the Wageningen University as a researcher and lecturer. He has taught courses on project management and has been involved in several large-scale supply chain development projects in the agribusiness.